BUCKSKINS
AND
BLACK POWDER

Standin' Yer Ground
Dan "Buffler" Brewer

In a pen-and-ink drawing done especially for this book, Western artist Dan "Buffler" Brewer depicts two distinct styles of dress among the mountain men. The free trapper at left (a self-portrait of Brewer) wears garb fashioned in the mountains and showing strong Indian influence. The old boy has even re-armed himself with a flintlock rifle made for the Indian trade. The newcomer on the right (Roy Reynolds, founding member of the Southwestern Plainsmen buckskinning organization) is still wearing the clothes in which he crossed the Missouri, and he packs the most modern firearms to be found in St. Louis when he left.

BUCKSKINS AND BLACKPOWDER

A Mountain Man's Guide to Muzzleloading

KEN GRISSOM

Buckskinner portraits by Dan Brewer

Diagrams by Howard Paveglio

WINCHESTER PRESS

An Imprint of New Century Publishers, Inc.

Library of Congress Cataloging in Publication Data

Grissom, Ken.
  Buckskins and black powder.

  Bibliography: p.
  1. Muzzle-loading firearms.   2. Outdoor life.
I. Title.
TS536.6.M8G74   1982b   799.2'13   83-2193
ISBN 0-8329-0285-3

To Steve

Contents

David "Cripple Creek" Higginbotham.

Foreword

(To the tune of "Waiting for a Train")

Seven Mountain Men from Texas,
They all started on a ride.
They got the Har-O-The-Bar within
  them all
That cannot be denied.

They all do things the old way,
To them it is the best.
When it comes to living primitive
These men have stood the test.

Six were hard-core buckskinners,
One was a little green.
We call that boy SFB*
And the reason will be seen.

He's eaten rancid Possum,
He's eaten rotten Skunk,
He's ate week-dead Armadillo
No matter how it stunk.

When we finally made Fort Parker,
The Sheriff came to see us there.
The old folks had watched us ridin'
  through
And we caused them quite a scare.

But he did not arrest us.
He didn't lock us in his cell.
Don't think it's cause he liked us
  all,
But the way we'd begun to smell.

*Initials for a bawdy Indian name

He bade us all a good-bye,
And he said Y'all come again.
But if you do, please let me know
And I'll try to stay up-wind!

Then we rode back from Fort Parker
A hundred and thirty-five miles.
When we rode into the Ron-D-Voo,
Our faces were all smiles.

Then we fell off our horses
And the partyin' began.
Now I ain't lied about our ride,
But the story's at an end.

So let me tell you of these hearty
     souls,
And I'll tell you 'bout them all.
Let's start off with the biggest one
And work down to the small.

He said his name was Buffler,
And that we changed real soon.
After we spent one day with him,
He goes by Buffler Moon.

I'd like to tell his story,
I won't because I'm kind.
It don't have as much to do with
     the moon,
As it does with his behind.

Badger was our party leader.
And a good one he is, of course.
But he didn't count on the
     leadership
Of my crippled horse.

But I wouldn't want to slight him,
Let me bend your ear:
He's bound to be the best leader
     of all,
'Cause he can lead 'em from the rear.

And then we have this other man,
He's the one who wrote this book.
He's a helluva writer and Mountain
     Man,
But a gol-durned lousy cook.

Well he thinks he's a culinary
   genius,
But I've seen him a poison a few
When he cooked up a bunch of
   "wild onions,"
And put Death Camas in the stew!

Then there's a feller name of
   Two Bears
Who'll do anything for a show.
I've seen him fall plumb off his
   horse
And pose for a photo.

But why they call him Two Bears
Ain't never been plain to me.
Why should you call him Two Bears
When the man smells more like three!

Now I'll tell you about SFB,
And enough just can't be said.
That boy takes all our guff and
   then,
Heaps more upon his head.

He lost his food the first day
And after six days on the ride,
He'd a-fought for road-killed
   chicken snake
With wild onions on the side.

Black Kettle may be small in size
But he stands tall to me.
He walked part of the last thirty
   miles,
And fought the "Battle of
   Wounded Knee."

I call this man my brother
And I call him that with pride.
And if any feller ever was,
He's one with which to ride.

I'm *Kiúŋ nia Wókpana*,
That's Sioux for Cripple Creek,
I don't know why I told you
   'cause,
That language you probably don't
   speak.

Being Indian ain't just blood
   lines,
It's also in the heart.
If that's the case I'm more than
   fullblood
Indian from the start.

Now you know about a few of us,
So turn the page and look,
And you'll understand us a little
   more
By the time you've read this book.

If you feel someday you want to
   stray,
And sometime your heart gets weak,
Then come see me at Ron-D-Voo,
My name is Cripple Creek.

Yo te lay te oh!
Yo lay te oh!
Yo lay tee!

Cripple Creek

his mark

Preface

We were at a backcountry crossroad, taking a little break on the first day of a seven-day, 130-mile trail ride. Some of the guys were out to fulfill requirements for advancement in The American Mountain Men, so we were packing loaded muzzleloaders, prepared to do a little small-game hunting for food. And we had saddlebags stuffed with jerky, pemmican, hardtack, corn meal, salt pork, and other foods as would have been available to the mountain men of the early-to-middle nineteenth century.

Our saddles and tack were representative of the period, too, either handmade Indian types, or early southwestern styles reconstructed from old high-cantled trees, or modern replicas of the Santa Fe saddle. And of course we were decked out in buckskins and moccasins and the whole bit.

Along came a couple of guys on a tractor, and they were just about to fall off the thing, rolling with laughter. We had already garnered some strange looks, as you might suppose, but nobody had found us quite *that* amusing.

Buffler, one of our number, put our minds at ease. He came hiking back with a red face and a roll of authentic twentieth-century toilet paper in his hand.

There wasn't any cover around, but when you gotta go ... There weren't any people around either, except us, so Buffler had discreetly walked across the road and behind a tree. He was in plain sight of the guys on the tractor, though, and they saw him before they saw the rest of us. Lord only knows what they thought—here's this bearded bear of a man in an Indian shirt and a big hat with a feather in it, flashing his behind to the world. It just ain't the sort of sight a country boy expects to see while driving his tractor in Robertson County, Texas.

I'm telling you this story because there's a moral to it: No matter how authentic your gear or how sharp your primitive skills, you ain't about to shake the twentieth century.

I know a lot of buckskinners who view what they're doing as a brand of survivalism, like the people who dress up in camouflage coveralls and practice raking the potato patch with automatic-weapons fire to keep the neighbors out when the Big Crash comes. Most of the 'skinners, I must

Michael "Two Bears" Hughes enjoys playing Indian-fighter almost as much as his horse Sandy does, but they both know they're just play-acting. There is no way today to actually duplicate the hardships that the mountain men faced during the fur trade period.

say, are not all that stingy. In fact, item seven of the AMM code reads: "During any survival situation I shall be willing to divide any food and water I have and give any other assistance to people found in need." But many do honestly believe that when Armageddon cranks up, they'll just ease up into the hills and live the life of Jim Bridger.

Worse, some actually think they *are* mountain men!

Granted, many of the life-supporting techniques of the nineteenth-century trappers are valid today. Learn them and they will make you a better hunter and woodsman. The man, woman, or child who can cast himself into the bush with the simple artifacts of our forefathers and be relatively comfortable *is* doing something.

Some of today's 'skinners are as good as the old boys at striking a light with flint and steel or punching round balls through game, and at horsemanship, tipi etiquette, and so on. Some of them could even outclass the originals when it comes to sticking knives and tomahawks, or passing the jug one way and tall tales the other around a campfire.

But you could ride like the wind, drink like a moose, cuss like a tail-shot squirrel, and lie like a hot day on the desert. You still wouldn't be a mountain man.

There is no way to duplicate, in the twentieth century, the experience of having to shift for yourself a thousand miles deep in a vast wilderness peopled by an alien race, the friendliest of whom will steal you blind for the honor of it. The unfriendly ones are getting really nasty, your mule died yesterday, game is scarce, the weather's turning sour, you have a nagging cough and nothing to treat it with but oil of peppermint, and a grizzly's claw is unzipping the back of your lean-to.

If most of the hardships are gone, so are the highs—the grand feeling of letting your gaze drift over mile upon sparkling mile of uncharted wildnerness. The immense satisfaction of a bellyful of broiled buffalo hump-rib after weeks of wooden jerky and rancid pemmican.

Sure, you *can* find a better wilderness setting than a crossroad in Robertson County. But you would have to hire some Blackfeet to try to scalp you. And their hearts probably aren't in it anymore.

There are challenges in buckskinning, and a good 'skinner is a man or woman to be admired. But the old-timers who opened the way West deserve far more than to be ranked with the likes of us. All the real mountain men are dead. Their kind can never be again.

I tell you this in the hopes you'll be able to keep buckskinning in perspective. If, however, you go off the deep end ... well, it could be worse. The urban cliff dwellers who think the world is made of glass, concrete, and steel, and that it falls off into space beyond the Loop— they're the ones I really worry about. If a man has enough sense to yearn for a simpler and more natural life—never mind that it's unattainable—I say his heart is good.

Buffler's heart is good. He knows he has to work and buy insurance and pay taxes and mow the lawn just like the rest of twentieth-century America. But when it's time to relax, he'll pull on his buckskins, throw his Santa Fe saddle on ol' Star, and ride boldly down the side of the road, grinning ear-to-ear, as though he were going through South Pass for the first time ever. He'll be having fun.

And if it happens to amuse a couple of country boys from Robertson County, Texas, well that'll be fine.

Ken Grissom
Seabrook, Texas

Takin' a Pilgrim Under Yer Wing
Dan "Buffler" Brewer

In this drawing, "Buffler" Brewer illustrates one of the functions of the modern dog soldiers. Note the dog soldier's badge of office, the bands on the skinners' right arms. The man pointing out the sights is the artist himself. The second dog soldier is Fort Worth buckskinner Roy Reynolds, and the Texas cowboy is David Wilson, also of Fort Worth.

BUCKSKINS
AND
BLACKPOWDER

1

Muzzleloading's Big Comeback

There wouldn't be buckskinning today if the popularity of muzzleloading hadn't staged a big comeback. Yet that comeback is due in part to America's loyalty to its frontier heritage—that which makes us buckskinners, now that we have the guns. The relationship between muzzleloading and buckskinning has been more of a symbiotic one than a simple matter of one hobby spinning off another.

In the 1950's, before modern reproduction muzzleloaders were widely available, Walt Disney succeeded in putting a coonskin cap on the noggin of nearly every kid between four and fourteen. The Davy Crockett craze, remember? I was a 'skinner back then, boy, in my fringed split-cowhide jacket from Mexico and genuine rabbit-skin "coonskin" cap. They used to sell cheap moccasins off racks in the grocery stores like they do L'eggs now, remember that? I even made myself a muzzleloader with a piece of pipe fastened to a crude stock with a hose clamp. I had a pouring spout, taken from a box of salt, tacked over the breech area. It would lay forward, exposing a narrow channel in the wood through which I inserted a ladyfinger, with the fuse sticking out. After I lit the fuse, I pulled the spout back down to protect my face from the blast. That gun would sling a proper-size chinaberry a good ten yards, with a trajectory like an Acapulco cliff diver.

What appealed to me about the Davy Crockett series was the careful attention the Disney production gave to the firearms of the era. We kids were used to seeing cowboys shoot forty-eight times without reloading— and without hitting anyone, either, save maybe bruising a few fingers when one of those forty-eight shooters was *pling!*-ed from the grip of a black-hatted bad guy. The villain was always wrestled from the back of a plunging horse and brought to justice looking dusty and hateful, his greasy hair in ringlets and dark circles painted around his glaring eyes, but otherwise none the worse for wear.

You had to *reload* a Kentucky long rifle, we learned. And methodically,

3

with powder horn and ramrod. And the guns killed, bad guy and good guy alike. The juvenile mind perceived a real sense of history here, dark and bloody and heroic. We began to appreciate what sacrifices were made to bring our country into the twentieth century.

And we understood, maybe better than some adults do today, how tightly the civilian-owned firearm is woven into the fabric of our nation.

Another Disneyland series, *The Saga of Andy Burnett*, focused my

Slim Pickens, as Ol' Bill Williams in the Walt Disney series *The Saga of Andy Burnett*, convinced the author in his youth that there was something special about muzzleloaders.

attention for the first time on the Western Fur Trade Era. And when Slim Pickens, as Ol' Bill Williams, dropped to his knee and lit a fire with sparks off the frizzen of his rifle, there was cemented in me a conviction of the aesthetic superiority of muzzleloading firearms.

Other films are working the same magic on succeeding generations. The visually stunning *Jeremiah Johnson* with Robert Redford put a little polish on the Hawken image. And *The Mountain Men*, starring Charlton Heston and Brian Keith, is a wonderfully accurate look at the last days of the fur trade. The Civil War centennial in the sixties and the nation's big 200th birthday celebration in the seventies also contributed to the public's fascination with muzzleloading guns.

An exciting scene from *The Mountain Men*. Movies about the Western Fur Trade Era have contributed greatly to making the mountain man the most popular figure in buckskinning today. (Courtesy of Columbia Pictures)

A Practical Hunting Gun

And yet today, there are thousands of hunters who could not care less about the history behind their muzzleloading guns. They consider them to be tools to open the way to longer or more liberal deer seasons, or to help them recapture the long-faded thrill of hunting. The muzzleloading gun has been recycled. After a period of antique-relic-curio status, it is now considered a practical hunting gun again.

Historically, gunpowder's reputation as a game-getter was hard-earned. The ponderous 10-gauge arquebuses with their bothersome burning fuses were better suited to medieval standoffs at castle walls than to slinking through the forests of North America. But gunsmiths in Europe were tinkering with an ignition system that would create its own sparks on demand. Flint and steel had long been employed in the kindling of fires for cooking and heating. It was just a matter of time before the technology was applied to firearms. Rifling came along, too, as guns were put to more pleasant duties afield. In North America, however, hunting was more necessity than fun. German and Swiss settlers quickly modified their rifled flintlocks, called *jaegers*, to fit the realities of the American frontier.

The common jaeger had a bore around .60 caliber, but lead and powder had to be conserved in the New World. A .50-caliber rifle came a lot closer to meeting the needs of the American hunter. It still had enough power to put down a whitetail or an enemy, but it could be used on small game as well. The thirty-inch jaeger barrel grew by ten inches or more, which put the emphasis on deliberate aiming and tack-driving accuracy. At some point in the first half of the eighteenth century, the first true American firearm came into being. Although there are many subclassifications based on area and era, the general type is called the Pennsylvania (from the place it originated) or Kentucky (from the place it was used) rifle.

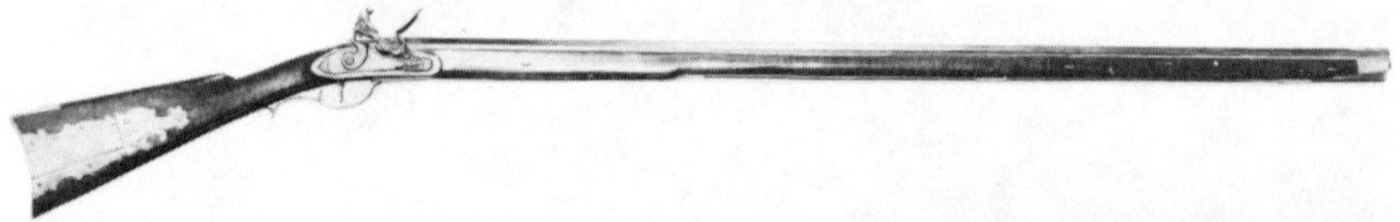

The mountain man's choice in the 1820s was likely to be a long-barreled flinter like this circa-1800 Kentucky rifle by Jacob Dickert of Lancaster, Pennsylvania. The plains rifle didn't come into wide use until the 1840s. (Courtesy of The Museum of The Fur Trade, Chadron, Nebraska)

As the frontier advanced across the wide Missouri, heavier game animals were encountered and longer distances were the norm. Also, riflemen were more frequently hunting from horseback. The resulting evolution in firearms produced the plains rifle with its typical large bore, shorter barrel, and heavy-wristed half-stocks. Meanwhile, the percussion system—in which a copper cup containing fulminate of mercury explodes upon being struck with a hammer, sending fire through a nipple port into the powder charge—was gaining favor over the flintlock. With the new system, the plains rifle was the peak of development in muzzleloading rifles.

These Hawkens, Tryons, Lemans, etc., served the westerners well in the 1840s and 1850s. Military armament had kept abreast, and the War

Between the States in the following decade was fought largely with guns that loaded through the muzzle, but the new breechloaders grabbed the limelight. The 1870s was the decade of the Winchester '73, the Sharps Old Reliable, Colt Peacemaker, and Smith & Wesson American. Just when they were getting good, muzzleloaders seemed doomed to a dusty corner of the past.

The Sport of the Future

Muzzleloading never died out altogether. The embers were kept barely burning by a handful of diehards and were finally fanned back into flame by an even smaller number of entrepreneurs—guys like Turner Kirkland and Val Forgett, who knew the old ways still had a place in the hearts of American shooters.

At first, however, muzzleloading survived out of necessity rather than nostalgia. In the hardscrabble Appalachians, for example, folks kept making and hunting with versions of the Kentucky rifle now called "poor boys" or southern mountain rifles. It was cheaper to buy bulk powder and cast your own balls than buying cartridges and the new cartridge-firing guns. Besides, the front-stuffers had always brought home the bacon.

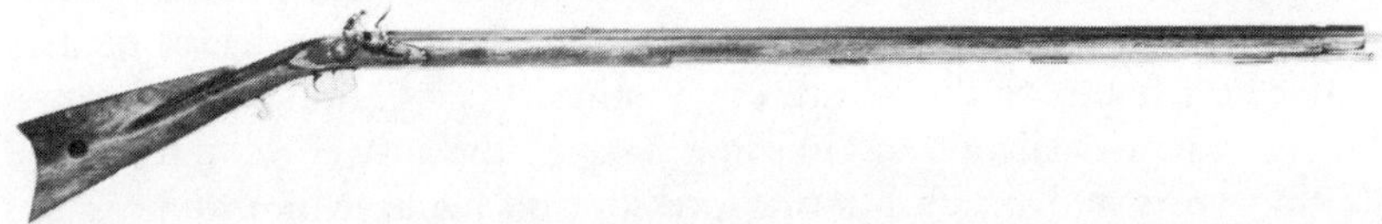

Dixie Gun Works Tennessee Mountain Rifle, an excellent reproduction of the "poor boy" Kentucky rifle. (Courtesy of Dixie Gun Works)

That the old guns were more than adequate in the field was something a later generation of shooters discovered accidentally, by taking grandpa's old shootin' iron down from over the mantle and wringing her out behind the barn. For them, the muzzleloading renaissance began as just plain fun.

As the years spun on into the smokeless-powder age, there grew a nostalgia, a longing for the good old days, and some folks shot muzzleloaders just to keep the art alive, the way old ladies in dairy country get together and churn butter. In the National Rifle Association's *American Rifleman* magazine, February 1931 issue, there appeared this notice:

An event for muzzle-loading rifles only, with none of the gadgets for fancy sighting, is now being promoted by Mr. Oscar L. Seth, president of the N. & W. Ry Y. M. C. A. Rifle and Revolver Club of Portsmouth [Ohio]. Seth knows the location of many a fine old gun of ramrod loading and claims that an annual competition, with suitable prizes, will bring them out and have men behind them that can show the present-day crop of riflemen a thing or two.

That little gathering grew into the National Muzzle Loading Rifle Association, set up to oversee muzzleloading target shoots, as the NRA does for breechloaders. The NMLRA, which now has about 25,000 members, is also involved in buckskinning, hosting three major rendezvous and setting aside a primitive camp at the big national shoot at its Friendship, Indiana, headquarters.

If there are 25,000 members in one organization, think of all the local clubs with no national affiliation. And there must be many thousands more plinking away with guns made from kits, hunting or even buckskinning completely on their own. Frankly, no one knows for certain how strong muzzleloading is today. Manufacturers and importers are reluctant to pool their sales figures, presumably because they fear it would look like a welcome mat for federal regulation. But the popularity of the sport is obvious. Colt was reintroducing its cap-and-ball revolvers while discontinuing its cartridge single-actions. The Japanese are in the marketplace with the Charles Daly line of front-stuffers. Dixie Gun Works is shipping almost as many catalogs as L.L. Bean. Gun stores and even department stores and discount houses are stacking Thompson/Center Hawkens and Renegades alongside the Remingtons and Winchesters.

More than just another facet to the shooting sports, muzzleloading may be the best hope for the future of shooting. It gives hunters and target shooters a new challenge and in some cases it's the answer to overcrowded hunting areas and heavy hunting pressure on game. More hunters can safely work a given acreage when they're armed with relatively low-power, close-range guns than when they're carrying high-power centerfire rifles. And hunters are usually satisfied with a smaller bag when they've taken game the old-fashioned way.

You Are What You Shoot

The difference between the gathering of a few codgers in neckties and porkpie hats in the 1930s and the broad-gauged appeal of muzzleloading today has been the influx of a massive and steady supply of modern muzzleloading guns at prices the average shooter can afford. Much of the credit for that belongs to Turner Kirkland and Val Forgett for sticking their necks out and testing the market.

It was a labor of love for both men. Kirkland was one of the fellows who started shooting the originals, and his hobby grew into a small business when he began to stockpile parts to help others keep their charcoal-burners in action. Then in 1955, when America was still in the grips of the

Davy Crockett craze, Kirkland imported a Belgian-made .45-caliber long rifle he dubbed the Dixie Squirrel Rifle. It was an immediate success, but just a taste of what was to come.

"In 1956 we sold three or four hundred of those guns," Kirkland said, "and today that's nothing!" If he could keep the Tennessee Mountain Rifle (a careful reproduction of the "poor boy" Kentucky) in stock at his Union City, Tennessee, warehouse, Kirkland said he could easily sell several thousand a year.

Forgett—whose efforts spawned Navy Arms Co. of Ridgefield, New Jersey—tackled another aspect of the sleeping black-powder market. He sent an original Colt 1851 Navy revolver to the arms manufacturing center of Brescia, Italy, and produced the first of many replicas to enter the U.S. market. Today, Navy Arms can furnish you with replicas of cap-and-ball Colts from the Paterson to the 1863 Sheriff's Model, and a host of other historic firearms like the U.S. Rifle Model 1803—the Harper's Ferry rifle of Lewis and Clark fame—and the Henry repeater, that "damn Yankee gun that can be loaded on Sunday and fired all week long!"

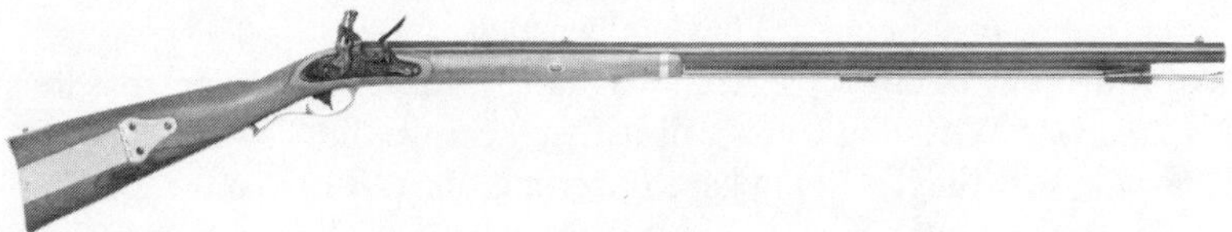

Navy Arm's copy of the U.S. Rifle Model 1803, the Harper's Ferry rifle carried on the Lewis and Clark expedition. This replica comes in .58 caliber instead of the .54 caliber of the original. (Courtesy of Navy Arms)

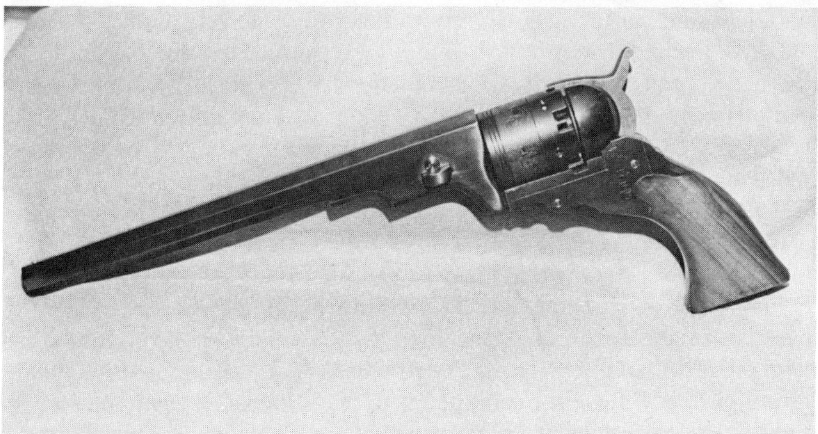

Although Paterson Colts may have been in circulation as early as 1836, there almost certainly weren't any at the mountain rendezvous. But the Taos trapper Kit Carson had one by 1841, and they are accepted sidearms at today's primitive gatherings. This one is an original. (Photo by Bill Thompson, courtesy of *The Houston Post*)

Dixie Gun Works and Navy Arms are but two among many nowadays, albeit two of the best known. Some newcomers merely jumped on the bandwagon and are cranking out cap-and-ball revolvers and plains rifles with the best of 'em. There are still innovators, though. Thompson/Center Arms of Rochester, New Hampshire, certainly qualifies. The T/C Hawken draws a lot of criticism from buckskinners for its lack of resemblance to its namesake, but it is nonetheless the most popular muzzleloading rifle in America, probably by a comfortable margin. Its illegitimate lines aside, it deserves a lot of the credit for interesting the black-powder public in plains rifles and the era of the mountain men.

The T/C Hawken was only incidentally associated with the famous product of Sam and Jake Hawken anyway. It was intended to be a strong, reliable hunting gun with its adjustable sights, modern coil-spring lock, and the fast, shallow rifling suited for conical bullets. And while it was patterned after a nineteenth-century gun, it wasn't a plains rifle but an eastern sporter owned by Warren Center.

"I just more or less beefed up the New England half-stock that I had," he said, "made it a bigger caliber and made it a little heavier, and really had no intention of producing a 'Hawken' as such.

"And then one of our reps, from Missouri I think, said, 'Jeez, that looks like a *Hawken!* Why don't you call it that?' So we did."

It's ironic that the T/C Hawken, unacceptable as it is to most 'skinners, really opened people's eyes to the Hawken legend. And as I mentioned earlier, it led many of us down the trail toward buckskinning.

I acquired a .50-caliber T/C Hawken just for deer hunting, although there's no special incentive for using a muzzleloader in Texas beyond the pure fun of it. I shot Maxi-Balls in it for a while, but hanging around other muzzleloading enthusiasts, I grew to favor the patched round ball. The old-style loading just appealed to me. I recognized that the long bullet is the better projectile for hunting, but for Texas whitetails within eighty yards, the round ball is more than adequate. I even shunned Pyrodex while at the same time acquiescing to the advantages of "replica black powder."

To make a better round-ball gun of my Hawken, I had Houston gun-maker J.B. Tabor recut the rifling to .012 inch, went to a .495 ball and pillow ticking for patching that mikes out at .019. Made a tackdriver out of it.

Phony pedigree or not, it's still my numero uno deer gun. I never did like that blued barrel, so Chris Hirsch—the young Houston gunmaker who presented an ornate Kentucky rifle to President Reagan—browned it nicely for me. But then I equipped it with a sling and a modern receiver sight. It doesn't belong at a rendezvous, but it can sit in a tree with me any November.

With that kind of attitude, you would think I would have been safe from buckskinning fever. I wasn't and you ain't, either. That T/C Hawken had thrown me in with bad company. Ere long I was tanning hides and making moccasins, chunking a 'hawk in the backyard, and, alas, going to rendezvous. You'll know what's happening to you when you start shying away from Maxi-Balls and Pyrodex.

I have, however, retained something of an ability to "float" my sense of authenticity to match the occasion. I hunt with the T/C, as I mentioned. When I soldier with the Texas Army, a Texas Revolution reenactment group, I carry a Trails Gun Armory "Alamo Long Rifle," patterned after an original now on display in that famous fortress. Because it has the seal of the State of Texas engraved on the patchbox, among other things, the "Alamo Long Rifle" isn't strictly authentic. But spectators at Army doin's don't look that closely, and the gun certainly fits into the spirit of things.

My hard-core, rendezvousing artillery is a Hirsch-made London fusil that Chris put together from North Star parts with Charles Hanson's excellent work, *The Northwest Gun*, at his elbow.

That's how you get into this deal, in stages.

"We watch a guy come in and buy his first kit one year," said Art Ressell of The Hawken Shop, St. Louis. "The second year he comes in and modifies it, gets custom parts and so forth. The third year, if he's stayed with it, he wants a custom rifle and he's looking around for a war shirt and that type of thing."

Something For Everybody

"The muzzleloading rifle stirs an interest in the history behind it," said John Baird of Big Timber, Montana, editor and publisher of *The Buckskin Report* and founder of the National Association of Primitive Riflemen.

"Most of the time the type of rifle a person favors will determine the portion of history they get most interested in. If they're long rifle enthusiasts, they get interested in the American Revolution or the Old Northwest. If they have a plains rifle, the Jim Bridger and Liver-eatin' Johnson sort of thing."

Right now the vast majority of buckskinners are dedicated to recreating the days of the mountain men. If Baird is right, that could be largely due to the extreme popularity of the plains rifle (historically correct or not; see Chapter 4). Yeah, that includes the T/C Hawken. But who knows which way the wind will blow next? Interest in the Old Northwest—an earlier period of the fur trade centered around present-day Illinois, Indiana and Ohio—is coming on. The Wild West of the 1870s has always had its aficionados, as have the Civil War and American Revolution. There is even the slightest of drifts toward the black-powder days in Africa.

Mike Powasnick of Trail Guns Armory, League City, Texas, was

Buckskinning is now a big part of the activities at National Muzzle Loading Rifle Association shoots. These 'skinners attending the national championships at Friendship, Indiana, are on their way to the mountain man run course, a sort of primitive FBI drill. (Photo by John Wootters)

thinking along the same lines as Warren Center when he designed his .58-caliber Kodiak double rifle. He wanted a gun similar to the English percussion doubles used in Africa during the 1850s, but above all, an efficient hunting gun. He took his design to the Italian firm of Davide Pedersoli, and with the prototype put his dream to the supreme test in South Africa and Zimbabwe, dropping cape buffalo without the help of his professional hunters' .458 Winchester Magnums.

Powasnick, who has had a muzzleloading-only deer lease in Texas for more than twenty years, believes that the pressure on hunting in Africa could be eased by the use of muzzleloaders. Certainly it would present a greater challenge for Bwana. At this writing, Powasnick and black-powder writer Rick Hacker were planning another muzzleloading hunt in Africa, this time in nineteenth-century safari garb. And it could be that someone will someday commission an old-fashioned foot safari and a whole new aspect of our fascinating hobby would be off and running.

"This is what I really like about the muzzleloading sport," said Oran Scurlock of Texarkana, Texas, publisher of *Muzzleloader* magazine, "there's an area of interest for just about anybody. If a fellow wants to be a Confederate cavalryman, he can be that. If he wants to be an eastern longhunter, he can be that. If he wants to be a western mountain man, he can be that. And if he doesn't care a thing about play-acting and is just interested in competitive shooting or hunting, he can do those, too.

"There's something for anybody and everybody who shoots a muzzleloader!"

2

The Western Fur Trade Era

The fact they get to carry plains rifles may be the major reason folks are attracted to the Western Fur Trade Era, but you must admit there's some awfully compelling history there, too. The events of that brief span of time drastically changed the nation and the world.

America grew up, got out of knee breeches, started sprouting whiskers, and took to electing professional politicians like Martin Van Buren instead of the likes of Citizen Thomas Jefferson.

The population of the United States more than tripled. Big Business was born. And Americans were calling the whole breadth of the continent home—all the way to the Pacific Ocean. Of course the big jump in territory came automatically with the Louisiana Purchase. But it was the mountain men who got the settlers looking westward, then showed them the way.

The Pathfinders

The mountain men were the tail end of a breed who had always been pushing westward, away from the grasp of civilization, since colonial days. Call them frontiersmen, pathfinders, leatherstockings, backwoodsmen, whatever, they were the people more at home in the wilderness than in the towns and cities. Rugged individualists, extremely self-reliant, they either "tamed" the Indians or ran them off altogether, then hunted and cleared tiny plots for corn, cotton, tobacco.

The leatherstockings frequently found themselves second-class citizens when the land they had won began filling up with farmers, merchants, teachers and preachers, bankers, lawyers, smiths—the agents of commerce, society, and government. Like a rising tide, the wilderness became the United States, and the average backwoodsman found himself short on Dan'l Boone's elbow room and maybe a little long on unpaid taxes and dry-goods bills. So he would pack up his meager belongings and with a long rifle in the crook of his arm, strike out once more into virgin territory. It happened over and over again until most of the country east off the Mississippi was civilized.

That was forest land, though, and the leatherstockings were a forest people, bound to a rudimentary agriculture. What we now call the Great Plains, they reckoned to be desert—the "Great American Desert" it was called right into the gold rush. If it hadn't been for Napoleon Bonaparte, the westward expansion of the United States might have been checked for good.

The Louisiana Purchase

Spain held the Southwest, but Spain was in rapid decline and posed no threat to the United States. In the Northwest, along the western fringe of the Indiana Territory, the British and Canadians were becoming troublesome. The lucrative fur trade had gravitated to that part of the continent, pitting Americans against their northern neighbors. There was the strong suspicion that the Canadian North West Company, successor to the old French trading posts along the Missouri, was deliberately setting the Indians against U.S. interests. And a British push to colonize the West seemed inevitable.

But the immediate problem was down on the Gulf of Mexico. New Orleans, while on foreign soil, was nonetheless vital to commerce in the United States' Mississippi Territory, Tennessee, Kentucky, and on up into the Indiana country. And New Orleans, which had been under Spain's weak hand, was suddenly being deeded over to France.

France was Napoleon. And Napoleon was *real* trouble.

He was busy trying to conquer Europe at the time, but the Little Dictator evidently still had designs on the Americas. He had a sugar empire cooking on Santo Domingo, in the West Indies. When the plantation hands revolted, he sent a force to make things cool again in the Caribbean. Pulling men out of the fighting in Europe meant Napoleon was willing to make a serious investment in Santo Domingo; he would surely welcome the resources of the American West to help support his efforts.

The specter of Napoleon Bonaparte in the heart of North America was chilling, especially for the new president, Thomas Jefferson. The first concern was that Napoleon would halt U.S. commerce on the Mississippi. So Jefferson sent James Monroe to Paris to try to buy New Orleans from Napoleon. His timing was excellent. He arrived in France about the time Napoleon learned his military expedition to Santo Domingo had failed, bringing the demise of the sugar empire. Without Santo Domingo, the wilderness of Louisiana meant little to France. So Napoleon unloaded the whole region on Monroe for sixty million francs, to be spent in conquering the world.

Monroe, remember, was sent to buy New Orleans. He came home with a deed to all the land between the Gulf of Mexico and the upper reaches of the Missouri, between the Mississippi and the Rockies. It caused a big stink. People still had the idea the whole West was one big desert.

For the first time in history, the frontier of the United States had advanced beyond its frontiersmen. And if it had been up to the hunters and subsistence farmers who had settled the country's Near West, the British might still have wrested away the remaining part of the continent. The traditional borderers were stopped cold; there was a little *too* much elbow room across the wide Missouri.

The Fur Trade

So it wasn't for new lands with tall timber and plenty of game that the new territory was peopled—it was for beaver.

By 1803, beaver was the staple of the fur trade. Textiles had become available and the demand for skins and furs for clothing had fallen off. But beaver fur was still the only material suitable for making felt, and felt hats were all the rage. The fur and outer layer of hair were shaved from the dried beaver pelts, or plews, and then matted, soaked with glue, and molded into cocked hats, naval bicornes, fancy top hats and plain flat-brimmed ones. By the 1830s, when the mountain trade was in full swing, about a hundred thousand plews a year were being turned into hats.

One of the tasks Jefferson assigned Meriwether Lewis and William Clark on their historic trek across the Louisiana Purchase was to keep an eye peeled for beaver. He knew the nation's security would benefit from Monroe's land deal, but it would be nice if its citizens could turn a buck there as well. Lewis and Clark, as you might guess, found plenty of beaver sign.

The mountain country was already ringed with fur traders—Americans on the Missouri to the east, Britons and Canadians to the north and

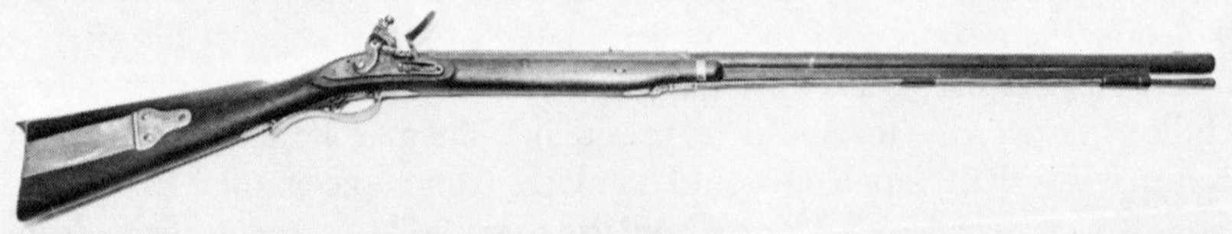

An original U.S. Rifle Model 1803. This half-stock big bore with its relatively short barrel was the forerunner of the plains rifle. (Photo by Bill Thompson, courtesy of *The Houston Post*)

northwest, Spaniards to the south. The trade had traditionally relied on the Indians to do the actual harvesting of pelts. The traders would build posts—the U.S. government got into the act with its "factories"—to which the Indians would come and exchange pelts for guns, knives, hatchets, kettles, cloth (pretty wonderful stuff if you can imagine living without it), and such foofaraw as beads and mirrors. The trade altered the economies of the tribes of the Old Northwest in the Indiana and Ohio country almost as much as the horse did on the plains. The Indians became rabid consumers, as mesmerized by the stock of goods in the posts as we today are by the hype of Madison Avenue.

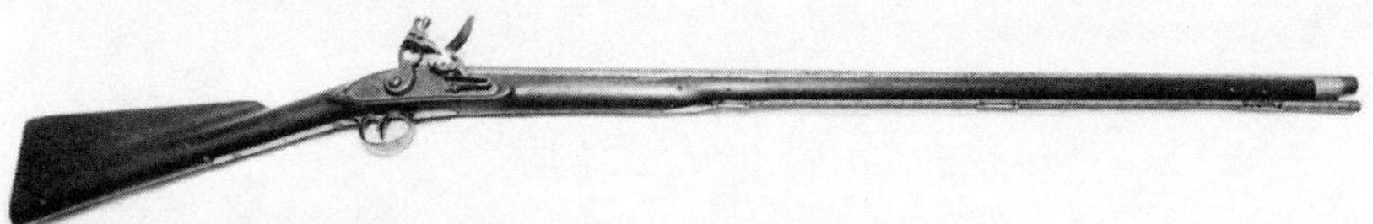

Model 1807 Springfield musket, a typical trade gun designed for Indian consumers. (Photo by Bill Thompson, courtesy of *The Houston Post*)

They abandoned their status as the nation's first conservationists and became market hunters. And they were spurred on by the traders, whose own ideas of conservation were overshadowed by competition—the Hudson's Bay Company, North West Company, various U.S. outfits, and the government factories. Soon the Old Northwest began to peter out and attention was focused on the rim of the "Great American Desert."

The Missouri country had been a trading center for different Indian cultures way back into the dim past, and there were whole villages of aboriginal businessmen living on its banks. The river was an excellent means of supplying the traditional posts of the white men. And from as deep in the new land as the whites traveled, there were tales of an abundance of beaver.

In 1806, one of Lewis and Clark's hunters, John Colter, was mustered out of the returning Corps of Discovery to trap the Grand Teton and Yellowstone regions, becoming the first legendary mountain man. In 1807, Manuel Lisa, a St. Louis trader, built a fort at the mouth of the Big Horn River in present-day Montana. By 1809, the North West Company had posts at Pend Oreille Lake in Idaho and in the Flathead country of Montana.

A partner in Lisa's St. Louis Missouri Fur Company, Andrew Henry, established a post at the confluence of the Jefferson and Madison rivers, east of what is now Butte, Montana in 1810. The next year, he crossed the Continental Divide and built a post on a fork of the Snake River north of the modern city of Idaho Falls.

John Jacob Astor's Pacific Fur Company—a branch of his American Fur

Company of Old Northwest fame—went around by sea and, in 1811, established a post at the mouth of the Columbia River on the Oregon coast.

The U.S. Army had, by 1808, even built Fort Osage near what is now Kansas City. With army protection and the underlying implication that other government support would be forthcoming, it looked as though the Rocky Mountains would soon be just another theater of multi-national competition, with the Taos and Santa Fe traders joining in the pie-slicing.

Not so. Westward expansion was still politically unpopular in the United States, and Napoleon's war in Europe stymied the economic incentive for everybody.

The War of 1812

Europe was the primary market for American furs, and hostilities between Great Britain and France were draining much of Europe's disposable income, putting luxuries like a new beaver hat on the back burner. Real and paper blockades were tactics of the war and American shipping was caught in the middle. Only at the greatest difficulty and expense could Yankee traders get pelts to the dwindling European markets, and get European-made trade goods back to the Indian fur hunters.

Finally, the United States actively entered into the hostilities in protest of the high-handed manner with which the British had been treating American merchantmen. Moreover, the old suspicion that the British were doing more than just arming the redskins—that they were inciting them and actually leading them to battle—had begun to ring true. Under seige, Fort Osage was closed in 1813. And Astoria, the Pacific Fur Company's settlement on the Columbia, was surrendered to the Canadian North West Company.

The western fur trade was at a standstill and westward expansion was out of the question.

After the War of 1812—which, if we didn't win we didn't lose either—things began to improve. Fort Osage was reoccupied. A new one, Fort Atkinson (near present-day Omaha), was raised. Altogether, fourteen hundred troops were assigned to the West. With military protection, with markets and the supply of trade goods renewed, the St. Louis traders stepped quickly back into business-as-usual along the Missouri.

"Great American Desert"

But attitudes hadn't changed among the frontier stock who had settled the lands to the east. They were still a forest people, and although the Lewis and Clark reports had accurately described the grandeurs of the new land, the troublesome adjective "treeless" kept popping up. Lieutenant Zebulon Pike had taken the less-than-scenic route into the West, crossing the badlands of what are now Kansas, Colorado, New Mexico, and Texas, and in 1810 he reported seeing "tracts of many leagues where the wind threw up sand in all the fanciful forms of the ocean's rolling waves and on which not a speck of vegetable matter existed.... Farms in the West will be limited to the banks of the Missouri and Mississippi, and the prairies, unfitted for cultivation, must be left to the wandering and uncivilized aborigines."

There were those—chiefly those who had no intention of leaving their comfortable beds—who heard the call of Manifest Destiny, and the issue of westward expansion became a political hot potato. Some folks argued that the United States had no business with colonies, and few could warm to the idea of granting full statehood to areas peopled mostly by savages. A military plan to explore the Yellowstone region to "enlarge and protect our fur trade and bring permanent peace to our northwestern frontier" was diverted to the Colorado badlands and Major Stephen Long came back with a report that appeared to confirm the old myth of a "Great American Desert." Every year between 1820 and 1824 there was an attempt in Congress to create a territory of Oregon, and every year it failed.

So if anyone was going to open the West, it would have to be the fur men themselves. It was no short order. The trading-post method so successful in the Old Northwest was breaking down. The vast hiatus of the Great Plains made it difficult to supply a post year round, and the inhabitants of the new land were uncooperative to say the least. Lisa and Henry had to close their posts because of trouble with the Blackfeet.

The Mountain Men

John Jacob Astor was willing to head west again. After successfully lobbying for an end to government competition in the fur trade (i.e., the factory system which had been a thorn in his side in the Old Northwest), Astor opened the doors of a New American Fur Company office in St. Louis. It was 1822, the dawn of a new era.

In that same year, Lisa's old partner, Andrew Henry, and General William Ashley placed an ad in the St. Louis *Missouri Gazette* calling for "100 men to ascend the river Missouri to its source," and attracting such future legend-makers as Jedediah Smith, Jim Bridger, and Hugh Glass.

Ashley and Henry had decided to do their own trapping in addition to what trade they could generate with the Indians. And after their boats were attacked by Arikaras in 1823, they struck out overland, Smith leading

Fort William, later called Fort Laramie, was founded by Bill Sublette and Robert Campbell to serve the fur trade. Situated in southeastern Wyoming, it later became a famous outpost on the Oregon Trail. The original structure, pictured here by Alfred Jacob Miller, was torn down in 1840. (Courtesy of The Walters Art Gallery, Baltimore, Maryland)

the first of many hooved caravans to penetrate the Rockies in the coming years.

They wintered with friendly Crows, cached supplies on the Sweetwater River in Wyoming in early spring, 1824, and crossed the Continental Divide at South Pass. The new mountain men scattered out and trapped the beaver-rich Green River area.

By the middle of June, they had all come back through the pass and rendezvoused at the Sweetwater cache. It was the practice run for the institution that would sustain the exploration and exploitation of the mountains, dispelling the "Great American Desert" myth and bridging the gap to the Pacific.

The annual rendezvous, beginning in 1825 when Ashley resupplied his trappers at "Randavouze Creek" in the southwestern corner of present-day Wyoming, was where the mountain man unloaded his furs and obtained the supplies he needed to continue his wilderness life. In the 1830s, other outfits, including Astor's American Fur Company and dozens of free trappers, entered into the mountain trade. The rendezvous became sort of a free-wheeling business convention, complete with corporate spying and

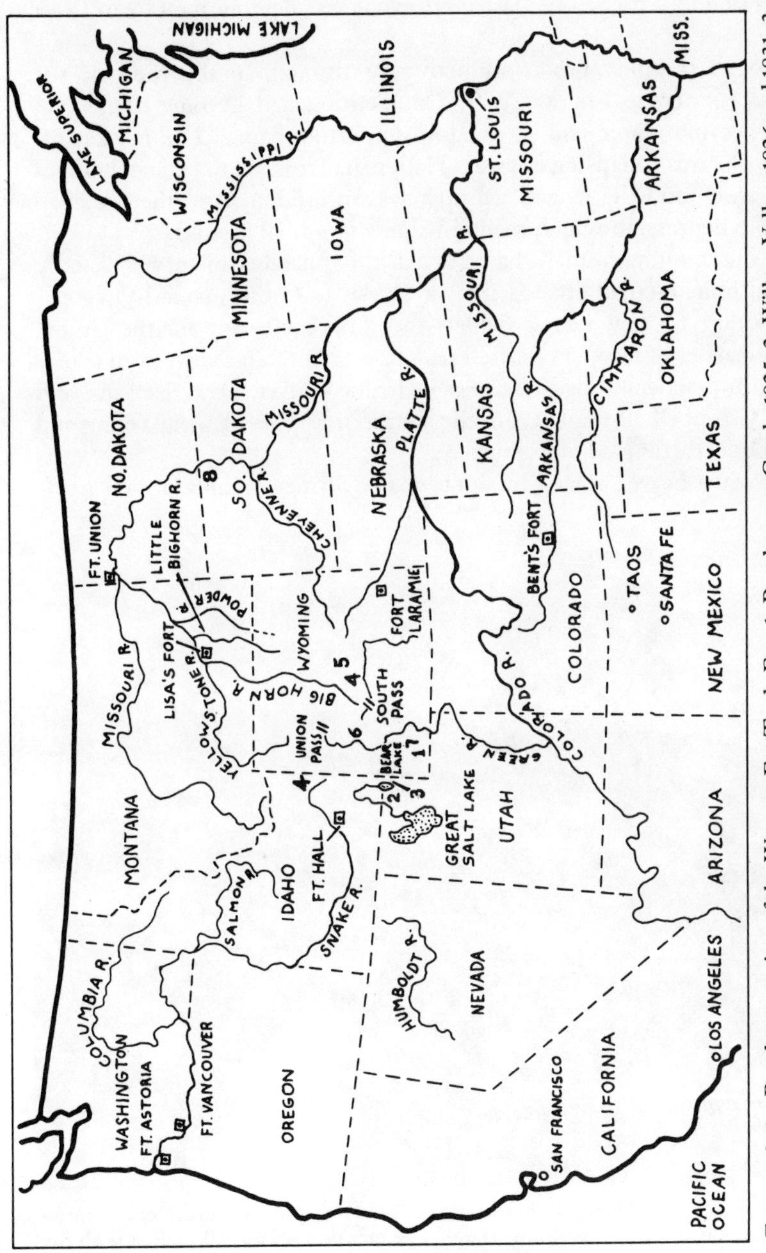

FIGURE 2–1 Rendezvous sites of the Western Fur Trade Era: 1. Randavouze Creek, 1825; 2. Willow Valley, 1826 and 1831; 3. Bear Lake, 1827 and 1828; 4. Pierre's Hole (west of the Continental Divide), 1829 and 1832, and Popo Agie (east of the Divide), 1829 (rendezvous was held in two parts); 5. Wind River, 1830 and 1838; 6. Green River, 1833, 1835, 1836, 1837, 1839, and 1840; 7. Ham's Fork, 1834. The Arikara attacked the 1823 Ashley-Henry expedition near 8. and forced the overland route that led to the rendezvous system.

efforts to bribe away the services of free trapper and company man alike. In later years, it was a way station for missionaries, adventurers, and Oregon-bound settlers. The last rendezvous was held on the Green River in 1840.

Although trapping has continued right through to the present, the Western Fur Trade Era was over. Competition had become too fierce. Beaver became scarce and so did life-supporting game. The market for beaver pelts was collapsing anyway. Hatters had learned to make felt out of sheep's wool, and the new silk topper was in fashion. And there was an economic depression which made business tough all around.

But the mountain man had served the purpose history belatedly assigned him. He had opened the way West, to California and Oregon.

To explore for new beaver fields—and some say to spy for the United States—parties of trappers crossed real deserts to reach the western shore. Jed Smith practically made a career of it. Joe Walker, Davy Jackson, and Robert Campbell all went. From the southern Rockies, Ewing Young and James Ohio Pattie made the journey.

And when beaver ceased to shine, many former mountain men made

Charlton Heston and Brian Keith, in *The Mountain Men*, portray old-timers witnessing the decline of the mountain fur trade. The movie is set in 1838, when both fur prices and beaver populations had fallen off. (Courtesy of Columbia Pictures)

their homes in California and Oregon, some of them using their finely honed fighting skills in the Bear Flag Revolt. Others put their talents to use along the Oregon Trail, scouting and hunting for the wagon trains, and setting up supply posts. Still others went to work for the army, or became buffalo hunters.

The Wild West of a million paperbacks and horse operas was just beginning. But the real wild times were over.

3

"A Majority of Scoundrels"

At some early point in your buckskinning career, you should take careful stock of *your* role as a modern mountain man. Recreating the past is more fun if you have a script in your head and a part sorted out for yourself, all based on the brief history of the mountain fur trade. It makes the rendezvous come to life, a real voyage back through time instead of a masquerade party.

Mountain men varied widely in character and personality. There was the efficient and pious Jed Smith, the jolly Joe Meek, the drunken Lucien Fontenelle, the born-in-slavery Jim Beckwourth, and the royal-born William Drummond Stewart. There were Britons and black men and French Canadians and Mexicans and even Indians among the full-fledged mountain men. Many Delawares had been fur hunters in the Old Northwest, and when it played out they picked up stakes and moved west with their white counterparts.

Not all mountain men were fur trappers. Some of the most famous names of the era actually did very little trapping at all. They were entrepreneurs who employed their own trappers and traded for the pelts of others, or else they were field agents for businessmen based back east. These agents were called *bourgeois* or "booshways," when they held command at a trading post or presided over a rendezvous, and "partisans" when they led trapping or exploring expeditions.

Even among the trappers there were stark differences. They were classed basically as either company men, who worked for wages and used company-owned equipment, or as free trappers, independent business-men who restocked their supplies by trading fall and spring furs to the highest bidders. Among the free trappers was a subclass known as "skin trappers," men who were more-or-less under contract to the companies. A skin trapper would be grubstaked by a company and was therefore obliged to trade with that company.

The Mountain Men, filmed with hard-core buckskinners as extras, accurately depicts the later years of the fur trade. Here, Charlton Heston leans on a customized plains rifle with a Thompson/Center-style capbox, and Brian Keith cradles a Dixie Hawken Percussion. Genuine Hawkens would have been a rare sight at the original rendezvous. (Courtesy of Columbia Pictures)

The Free Trapper

The pure free trapper is the historic figure we're usually thinking of when we think of the mountain man. He was the one closest to the Indians, frequently taking an Indian wife and maybe even being adopted into a tribe. He was the least likely to make any money out of the fur trade, but while he might barely keep body and soul together, he was the most princely figure in the mountains.

"The difference between a hired and a free trapper," said Meek through his chronicler, Francis Fuller Victor, in *The River of the West*,

was greatly in favor of the latter. The hired trapper was regularly indentured and bound not only to hunt and trap for his employers, but also to perform any duty required of him in camp. The

Pat "Badger" Kelly has carved out a role as a free trapper for himself. His breechclout and leggings and the smoothbore trade gun, studded with brass tacks, show strong Indian influence.

booshway, or the trader, or the partisan, had him under his command, to make him take charge of loading and unloading the horses, stand guard, cook, hunt fuel, or, in short, do any and every duty. In return for this toilsome service he received an outfit of traps, arms and ammunition, horses, and whatever his service required. Besides his outfit, he received no more than three or four hundred dollars a year as wages. There was also a class of free trappers, who were furnished with their outfit by the company they trapped for, and who were obliged to agree to a certain stipulated price for their furs before the hunt commenced. But the genuine free trapper regarded himself as greatly the superior of either of the foregoing classes. He had his own horses and accoutrements, arms, and ammunition. He took what route he thought fit, hunted and trapped when and where he chose; traded with the Indians; sold his furs to whoever offered the highest for them; dressed flauntingly, and generally had an Indian wife and half-breed children.

There were hundreds of free trappers in the trade toward the end. In fact, the southern Rockies, not rich enough in beaver to support the major operations, was almost entirely worked by free trappers out of Taos—men like Kit Carson, Joe Walker, and Ol' Bill Williams.

There also were adventurers like the wealthy Scots sportsman William Drummond Stewart among the serious beaver men. And government secret agents, some historians believe, who were testing Mexico's hold on California. And at the end there were missionaries and settlers using the rendezvous as a way station to Oregon.

There were, of course, women and children at the original rendezvous same as today. If they are going to be faithful to the history of the era, female and juvenile buckskinners are far more limited than male adults in their choices of roles. The gals can be Indians or the wives of missionaries; the kids can be Indians or half breeds.

"Good" Indians and Bad

Although the emphasis in the western mountains had turned away from the Indian trade and toward the non-Indian trapper, the tribes were still a major part of the rendezvous. They supplied some pelts, but also moccasins and other clothing, sleeping robes and some foods, and women, and the pageantry that has helped the rendezvous live in the imaginations of generations of later Americans.

Lewis and Clark made a good impression on the Flatheads and Nez Perces, whole villages of which were regular fixtures at the annual summer gatherings of the fur men. The Snakes, Utes, and Crows were also, to

There's no question as to the alter ego of the buckskinner on the left. The gent on the right is probably a free trapper, although he could be a company partisan or even a trader. Both 'skinners are participating in the NMLRA national shoot at Friendship, Indiana. (Photo by John Wootters)

some extent, friendly to the invaders. In the literature of the mountain fur trade, they come down as "good Injuns."

John Colter evidently got off on the wrong foot with the Blackfeet, villains of *The Mountain Men* and many another fur-trade drama. It could be that they were simply more jealous of their lands and more suspicious of the whites than their neighbors—sort of conservatives, you might say. In retrospect, it's hard to fault their position.

Many Indians today maintain a different perspective on those years than either Hollywood or the white man's history books portray. As they see it, their forebears flocked to the rendezvous because they had become enthusiastic consumers of civilization's tools and trinkets. You can imagine what a kettle meant to a woman accustomed to preparing meals in a buffalo paunch. They were also anxious to learn the white man's powerful "medicine." (The Methodists and Presbyterians interpreted this as a yearning for Christianity and they sent the first missionaries.)

This infusion of artifacts and ideas, beginning centuries earlier with the introduction of the horse, radically changed Indian economies and cultures. In the present-day Indian view, the new materialism among the tribes destroyed a highly spirtual, idyllic existence in which the red man was totally in balance with nature. (Read *Seven Arrows* by Hyemeyohsts Storm for the Indian historical perspective.)

The horse culture was deep-seated and many of the Indians of the West had already come into contact with a wide range of trade goods—via the ancient trading pipeline along the upper Missouri—by the time Lewis and Clark made their historic trek to the Pacific. The explorers distributed firearms and more goods among the natives they encountered. But most important was their very presence in the mountains. From that time on, there would always be non-Indians there.

Across the Wide Missouri

In August 1806, as the Lewis and Clark expedition made its way east again, the explorers ran into a pair of fur trappers who had been dogging their trail, Joseph Dixon and Forest Hancock. They were headed for the high country to begin the mountain man's craft. One of the expedition's best hunters, John Colter, was mustered out to join them. History doesn't have much to say about his partners, but Colter resurfaces again in the spring of 1807. Having seen the vast Yellowstone and Grand Teton regions, he was paddling back toward civilization alone when he ran across the fur trading expedition led by Manuel Lisa (and including other Corps of Discovery veterans George Drouillard, John Potts, and Peter Wiser) at the mouth of the Platte. Now a graduate mountain man, Colter's services were valuable to Lisa, and the crusty St. Louis trader convinced him to join them in another plunge into the wilderness.

Thus began the mountain fur trade, and in order to understand the mountain man, you need to be as aware of the fragile economy and turbulent politics of the trade as you are of the bouts with Indians and grizzlies, starvation and harsh weather.

Lisa and his partner, Andrew Henry, planned to utilize the trading-post system that had worked so well in the Old Northwest. But the Blackfeet were having none of it. The posts were abandoned and then everybody sat back to wait out the War of 1812.

Henry, with his new partner Ashley and their now-famous crew, had another go at it in 1822—this time evolving the celebrated and initially successful caravan method of supplying the trapping parties. Henry retired from the mountain trade in 1825, the year of the first true rendezvous, and Ashley took on the serious and competent youngster Jed Smith as a partner. The next year, Ashley sold out to Smith, Davy Jackson, and Bill Sublette, and concentrated his own efforts on the supply end of the trade.

The business of supplying the rendezvous, taking the year's pelts in trade, proved to be where the real money was. Although the prices given for furs in the mountains were artificially high during the years of intense competition, the markup on goods delivered there was even higher. By the time a free trapper resupplied himself with an "outfit," slaked his thirst for alcohol and bought a few trinkets to throw at the gals, he was lucky if he didn't find himself demoted to a skin trapper—or worse, a company man. Those who got rich in the fur trade, like Ashley and Sublette and Robert Campbell, were those who got into the supply business early on. The partisans and trappers wound up guiding wagon trains and scouting for the army—if they lived that long.

The new firm split up in 1831. Jackson went on to California. Sublette fooled around with the Santa Fe trade then, with Campbell, took over Ashley's supply service while the general concentrated on politics. Jed Smith headed for a rendezvous with destiny and a party of warring Comanches on the Cimarron.

Jim Bridger, Tom Fitzpatrick, and Milton Sublette (Bill's brother), along with Henry Fraeb and Jean Gervais, became the successors to the Ashley-Henry company. They called their firm the Rocky Mountain Fur Company (RMF Co.) but it became better known as "The Opposition" to John Jacob Astor's American Fur Company.

Astor, you may remember, had first tried to enter the western trade with the establishment of Astoria on the Pacific coast and had to abandon the post in the War of 1812. In 1822, he opened up shop in the West again, this time in St. Louis. Four years later he merged with the St. Louis firm of Bernard Pratte and Company; for the next five years, the American Fur Company—or simply "The Company," as it became known—limited itself to the upper reaches of the Missouri and the time-honored post system. But in 1831, a party of The Company under Lucien Fontenelle, Andrew Dripps, and Joseph Robidoux marched into the mountains for the first time.

It prompted several years of cat-and-mouse games with the more

Tom Fitzpatrick, depicted on his trap line by the painter Olaf C. Seltzer, founded the Rocky Mountain Fur Co. along with several other men. During the early 1830s, the RMF Co. and Astor's American Fur Company were in direct competition in the mountain fur trade. (Courtesy of The Thomas Gilcrease Institute of American History and Art, Tulsa, Oklahoma)

experienced men of the RMF Co., who led The Company's brigades into trapped-out valleys and, on at least one occasion, an Indian ambush. The Company retaliated by bribing away the services of RMF Co. employees and outbidding The Opposition for the plews of free trappers. It was probably this intrigue that caused the greenhorn Nathaniel Wyeth to label his fellow mountaineers a "majority of scoundrels."

In spite of the hard feelings between the groups, which, as the years went by, included the British Hudson's Bay Company, the camaraderie of the rendezvous apparently went unmarred. There were personal spats (the most celebrated of which was in 1835 when the diminutive Kit Carson silenced a big French-Canadian bully with a pistol ball), to be sure, but no pitched battles drawn along corporate lines.

Apart from its ruinous pricing policy, which even it couldn't afford finally, The Company had another ace up its sleeve. A black mountain man named Jim Beckwourth, an Ashley-Henry veteran, had been adopted by the Crows and was living among them as a chief of sorts. Working for The Company, Beckwourth helped engineer a change in the Crows' foreign policy. They became openly hostile toward their old friends of the

RMF Co.—not quite the threat the Blackfeet were, but definitely a hindrance.

With The Company at the same time becoming increasingly experienced in mountain craft, the pressure was too much. The RMF Co. folded and in 1834, Bridger, Fitzpatrick, and Milton Sublette briefly formed another partnership under contract to the American Fur Company. Finally, they abandoned it and went to work for The Company directly.

The Western Fur Trade Era still had five years to run, but it was all downhill on a steep grade.

"Beaver'll Never Shine Agin!"

The Mountain Men, a Columbia Pictures film, is an excellent study of the fur trade's decline. Shot in majestic Wyoming in the Bridger-Teton and Shoshone national forests and featuring the hard-core buckskinners of The American Mountain Men as extras, the movie *looks* right to begin with. And a lot of research is evident in the script written by Fraser Clarke Heston, actor Charlton's son.

It's 1838 and the St. Louis trade, such as it is, is dominated by The Company (which is now the partnership of Bernard Pratte and Pierre Chouteau, Astor having shrewdly bailed out several years earlier).

The annual rendezvous has been moved east of the Continental Divide, to the Popo Agie, probably to minimize the competition now coming hot and heavy from the Hudson's Bay Company. Many plews have nonetheless been diverted to the HBC post at Fort Hall on the Snake River, and the once-lively trading is a pretty somber scene. Trapper Bill Tyler (Charlton Heston), who missed the 1837 gathering, is astounded to learn that buffalo hides are going for more per pound than beaver. Trader Lucien Fontenelle (Ken Ruta) explains that the reason for it is on his head—a silk top hat, which has replaced felt toppers on the fashion scene.

The once-dashing mountaineers are creaky-kneed old-timers whose dreams of unexplored valleys rich in beaver are fading with their eyes. The mountains are trapped out; the hopeful faces at the rendezvous are those of the settlers bound for Oregon.

"Beaver'll never shine agin!" laments Bill Tyler.

Now the beaver hunting doesn't matter nearly as much as the simple fact that the mountain men were there, exploring the West and clearing the path to Manifest Destiny. Noting the trips fellows like Jed Smith and Joe Walker made to California in spite of many hardships and in light of increasing evidence that there were no beaver there, history buffs like to speculate that maybe they were really spies in buckskins. Maybe so. Walker, after all, was working for Captain B.L.E. de Bonneville, a U.S. Army officer on a curious leave of absence while he tried his apparently

The roles these 'skinners are playing are clear-cut: The fellow in the bib-front shirt is a free trapper with coon and beaver plews to trade; the guy in the tuque is a trader. The medium of exchange is the greenback dollar.

"Bourgeois Warrior and His Squaw," by Alfred Jacob Miller. According to Bernard DeVoto, this painting depicts the famed mountain man Joe Walker and his wife. (Courtesy of The Walters Art Gallery, Baltimore, Maryland)

woefully lacking skills as an entrepreneur in the fur trade. And Smith? Well, he had been the protege of Ashley, who in turn was the protege of Senator Thomas Hart Benton of Missouri, who was outspoken in favor of westward expansion.

The Literature

But that's one of the fun things about buckskinning, mountain man style: The history of the Western Fur Trade Era, played out as it was on so remote a stage, isn't exactly carved in stone. Letters, journals, newspaper accounts, bills of lading, and other sources are still being sifted through. And our picture of what the mountain man was, what his life was like, is still being painted.

Just as historians rely heavily on the eyewitness accounts that have come down to us—what they call "the literature" of the fur trade—so will you get a kick out of reading these frequently hair-raising (and sometimes hard to swallow) tales of the mountains. Beyond the enjoyment, you will learn a lot more about the daily life of a mountain man, and that *really* adds to your enjoyment when you try your hand at living that life yourself at the rendezvous.

The following is a basic list of the literature of the fur trade:

Adventures of Zenas Leonard, Fur Trader and Trapper: 1831–1836. The Burrows Brothers Company, 1904.

The Autobiography of a Mountain Man, 1805–1889, by Stephen Hall Meek. G. Dawson, 1948.

"The Correspondence and Journal of Captain Nathaniel J. Wyeth, 1831–36," in *Sources of the History of Oregon.* University Press, 1899.

The Diaries and Letters of Henry H. Spalding and Asa Bowed Smith Relating the Nez Perce Mission, 1838–1842, The Arthur H. Clark Company, 1958.

Forty Years a Fur Trader on the Upper Missouri: The Personal Narrative of Charles Larpenteur 1833–1872. F.P. Harper, 1898.

George Yount and His Chronicles of the West. The Old West Publishing Company, 1966.

A History of Oregon, 1792–1849, by William H. Gray. Harris & Holman, 1870.

James Clyman, 1792–1881. Champoeg Press, 1960.

Journal at Fort Clark, 1834–1839, by Francis Chardon. South Dakota Department of History, State of South Dakota, 1932.

"Journal of E. Willard Smith While with the Fur Traders, Vasquez and Sublette in the Rocky Mountain Region, 1839–40." Oregon Historical Quarterly, Vol. XIV, 1933.

Journal of a Trapper, by Russell Osborne. Oregon Historical Society, 1955.

Kit Carson's Autobiography. University of Nebraska Press, 1935.

The Life and Adventures of George Nidever (1809–1883). University of California Press, 1937.

The Life and Adventures of James P. Beckworth as Told to Thomas D. Bonner. University of Nebraska Press, 1972.

Life in the Far West, by George Frederick Ruxton. University of Oklahoma Press, 1964.

Life in the Rocky Mountains: A Diary of Wanderings on the Sources of the Rivers Missouri, Columbia and Colorado from February, 1830, to November, 1835, by W. A. Ferris. The Old West Publishing Company, 1940.

Mountain Men: George Frederick Ruxton's First Hand Accounts of Fur Trappers and Indians in the Rockies. Holiday House, 1966.

"Old Letters from Hudson's Bay Company Officials and Employees, 1829–1840." Washington Historical Quarterly, Vol. II, 1909.

Peter Skene Ogden's Snake Country Journals. Hudson's Bay Record Society, 1971.

The River of the West (biography of Joe Meek), by Frances Fuller Victor. Columbian Book Company, 1870.
The Rocky Mountain Letters of Robert Campbell. Frederick W. Beinecke, 1955.

Obviously you're not going to pick up many of these original source materials at your local bookstore. It calls for some heavy library work. There are many, many more historical works utilizing these sources and others (a few of them are found in the Bibliography) which are available at bookstores or by mail order through *Muzzleloader* magazine, *The Buckskin Report*, Dixie Gun Works, and others.

Another excellent source of information for 'skinners is *The Museum of the Fur Trade Quarterly*, published at Chadron, Nebraska. Editor and museum director Charles Hanson is one of the nation's foremost authorities on the everyday activities of the mountain fur trade. Hanson's work and the museum are supported in part by memberships (annual dues at this writing are $4), which include a subscription to the MFT Quarterly. For more information, write the museum at Route 2, Box 18, Chadron, Nebraska 69337.

Alfred Jacob Miller

Yet another excellent means of studying the dress, arms and equipment, and activities of the fur trappers and mountain Indians are the sketches and paintings of Alfred Jacob Miller.

Miller was contemporary to the perhaps better-known George Catlin and Karl Bodmer. But while Catlin and Bodmer preceeded him up the Missouri, Miller outdistanced them. He made it to Fort Laramie (Fort William) first, and he was the only artist to see the rendezvous.

Miller was there in 1837 at the invitation of Sir William Drummond Stewart, veteran of Waterloo, international sportsman, and eventual heir of some really old money. Stewart was about to set out on his fifth annual lark in the mountains during which he would entertain the mountaineers with wines and cheeses in his red-and-white striped tent at the rendezvous, then make a big-game hunting expedition before winter set in. And this time he wanted a pictorial record of the excitement and grandeur he had witnessed in past years. So he called on Miller at the artist's New Orleans studio and convinced him to come along.

Who knows what deliberation went into Miller's selection, but from the perspective of a century and a half, it seems a fortunate one. With his portrayal of action and use of color, Miller was what the people who know about such things call a "romantic" painter. Can you imagine a more romantic arena in which to work?

He wasn't afraid of detail, either, and for that above all else we

Sir William Drummond Stewart, a wealthy Scot who traveled through the Rockies, as sketched by Alfred Jacob Miller in 1837. Miller, the only professional artist to visit the rendezvous during its brief lifespan, came West at the invitation of Stewart, who wanted the excitement and grandeur of the mountains recorded. (Courtesy of The Collection of Western Americana, Beinecke Rare Book and Manuscript Library, Yale University, New Haven, Connecticut)

buckskinners thank him. Thanks to Miller, we know that mountain men wore whiskers and spurs and pucker-toe moccasins; that flintlocks were more common than caplocks; that saddles had narrow horns instead of big flat ones; and, for what it's worth, that Sir William had one hell of a beak.

Miller made hundreds of sketches, many of which were used as reference for the watercolors and oils he turned out until his death. And he took a volume of notes, which are in themselves of great value to the buckskinner-historian.

"Roasting the Hump Rib", by Alfred Jacob Miller. Besides making hundreds of sketches, Miller took voluminous notes about the life of the mountain men; today these make fascinating reading for enthusiastic buckskinner-historians. (Courtesy of The Walters Art Gallery, Baltimore, Maryland)

Consider Miller's eye for detail—and his sense of humor—in his notes on a sketch of the evening meal while the caravan was crossing the plains:

> A Trapper is … preparing that most glorious of all mountain morsels, "a hump rib" for supper.
>
> He is spitting it with a stick, the lower end of which is stuck in the ground near the fire, inclined inwards.
>
> The fire is often made from the bois de Vache ["wood" of the cow], but as we had the best of all sauces, viz, most ungovernable appetites, and most impatient dispositions for this same roasting operation, the circumstances did not affect us in the least. We found hunger so troublesome that it was quite a common thing to rise again at midnight and roast more meat, if we had any.

Miller lets us know that his recording of history was not without some sacrifice on his part.

> Every day at 12 noon the caravan halts, the horses are permitted to rest and feed, men receive their dinner, and then take a Siesta. The time however to me was too valuable to indulge in the luxury—so immediately after the halt, I would mount the wagon, get out my portfolio, and go to work. Our Captain [probably Tom Fitzpatrick], who took great interest in this matter, came up to me one day while so engaged, & said, "you should sketch this and that thing" and so on. "Well!" I answered, "if I had half a dozen pair of hands, it should have been done!"
>
> Capt: "That would be a great misfortune."
>
> "Why?"
>
> Capt: "It would be very expensive in the matter of kid gloves…."

4

The Guns of Buckskinning

Attractive as it is to amateur historians, buckskinning is primarily a shooting sport, and the muzzleloading gun is the centerpiece of the 'skinner's leisure-time activities.

Although most knowledgeable 'skinners will concede that the Hawken rifle did not play nearly as big a role in the mountain fur trade as was previously thought, the Hawken and Hawken-type (plains rifle, in other words) reproductions are still far and away the most popular firearms among the modern mountain men. 'Skinners *use* their rifles, and since the plains rifle represents the apex in the development of muzzleloading firearms, it's a smart choice for an all-around hunting gun. Many got into buckskinning in the first place at the urging of their Hawken reproductions, and if they had to become Forty-niners to remain faithful to 'em, by golly, they would!

The Hawken legend isn't dying, but it is being revised. Let's look first at how the development of firearms meshed with the Western Fur Trade Era, then we can go over the replicas and style reproductions available to the modern mountain man.

The first firearms on American soil in any quantity were big smooth-bored matchlocks. They were military weapons almost exclusively.

In Europe meanwhile, there was some crossbreeding going on between civilian sporting arms. The Germans had a rifled gun, rather awkwardly fired from the cheek and utilizing the reliable but expensive wheel lock as a system of ignition. The French, Dutch, and English were using the more plebeian flintlock on military muskets and civilian fowling pieces, all smoothbores. The Germans blended their large-caliber rifled barrels with the shoulder-mounted buttstock and the flintlock and came up with a first-class hunting arm, the jaeger.

The Kentucky Rifle

Early German, Dutch, and Swiss settlements in Pennsylvania sowed the New World with jaegers, planting the seed for the development of a truly American firearm. Calibers shrunk to conserve the scarce supplies of powder and lead. Barrels grew for more accuracy in taking the elusive woodland game. A major and lasting gunmaking industry grew up in Lancaster, Pennsylvania, but the American long rifle was soon being made just about anywhere there were concentrations of American frontiersmen.

It was the gun that won the dark, bloody ground of Kentucky and maybe for that reason alone it became known as the Kentucky rifle. Or you can assume the nickname came from a line in a very popular song written after the Battle of New Orleans:

> *But Jackson he was wide awake,*
> *And wasn't scared at trifles,*
> *For well he knew what aim we'd take*
> *With our Kentucky rifles.*

Never mind that it was the expert canoneering of Jean Lafitte's pirates far more than the sniping of the Kentucky hunters that won the Battle of New Orleans—a happy legend was struck.

Lewis and Clark had Kentuckies with them when they crossed the Rockies. So did many of the hearty souls who responded to Ashley's call for a hundred men at the opening of the mountain fur trade. Later on, the fur companies ordered Kentuckies by the gross from such Pennsylvania gunmakers as Leman, Deringer, Tryon, and Henry (who all later became better known for their plains rifles) to resupply company men and to trade to free trappers and Indians for furs.

To meet the demands of the mountain trade, the plains rifle was rapidly evolving. And other types of guns were available from the beginning. But historians now believe most mountain men stuck with the gun they knew best, the tried-and-true flintlock. The supply of caps for the new percussion arms was entirely dependent upon the annual trade caravan from St. Louis, but flint, or at least chert and agate, could be plucked right off the ground.

Charles Hanson, director of the Museum of the Fur Trade at Chadron, Nebraska, and author of *The Hawken Rifle: Its Place in History,* says if he must pick a "typical" mountain man's firearm, it's either going to be a southern-made "poor boy," or something like the stark "Lancaster pattern" trade rifle—both essentially Kentuckies.

Bill Tyler (Charlton Heston), in *The Mountain Men*, carries a flintlock Leman Indian rifle, a gun made for trade to the Indians and trappers living in the mountains. Ol' Bill or the Indian he took the rifle from has added rows of brass tacks to give the piece a little class. (Courtesy of Columbia Pictures)

The poor boy or southern mountain rifle (collectors call these Kentuckies "plain"—no *s*—rifles) is particularly interesting in light of Hanson's opinion that the Hawken half-stock shows marked southern influence. Poor boys can best be described as no-nonsense firearms. They were cheaply but not shoddily made. They came from the Appalachians where folks needed good guns and couldn't afford artwork. Stocks were simple.

Ornate patchboxes gave way to simple grease holes. Trigger guards and ramrod thimbles were of iron.

By the time the mountains were opened to trapping, Kentucky rifle barrels were still commonly beyond forty inches. And bore diameters reflected the relatively tame conditions in the East. *Flayderman's Guide to Antique American Firearms*, the collector's bible, calls .50 caliber the average in the first decade of the nineteenth century.

Jake Hawken, who preceeded his brother Sam to St. Louis from the family home in Maryland, was said to have initially produced big-bored Kentuckies for the new westerners.

The Plains Rifle

Eventually, the J&S Hawken product became known as *the* plains rifle. It was one of the best, no doubt about that. But it was neither the most common nor the first.

If you characterize the plains rifle as simply a half-stocked big bore, then a good argument can be made that the U.S. Government commissioned the first plains rifle, or at least a very early one, and sent it out with Lewis and Clark for field testing. The U.S. Rifle Model 1803 was a .54-caliber half-stock flinter with a 33-inch barrel, give or take an inch. It's tantalizing to speculate that maybe there were a few surplus M1803s kicking around St. Louis when Jake Hawken set up shop, and that Jake recognized a good idea when he saw one.

It soon became obvious to most, though, that larger calibers and shorter barrels were called for in the western trade. Travel was on horseback. And grizzlies, elk, and bison were no pushovers. Gunmakers like Leman started cranking out shortened, more potent Kentuckies—that is, plains rifles—for the trapper and Indian trade.

In the East, the trend was also toward shorter barrels and half-stocks, combined with the new percussion ignition system. Whether this trend, like so many others to come, was but a reflection from the West would be just a matter of speculation. But only the delicate proportions of their stocks and their relatively light calibers kept these "half-stock Kentuckies" from qualifying as true plains rifles.

Sometime before the end of the Western Fur Trade Era (1840), the Hawken brothers and some of the eastern manufacturers started making bona fide caplock plains rifles for use in the West. But the evidence is that, if these saw use in the mountains during the time of the rendezvous, it was in the hands of those few who could both afford them (Hawkens were expensive) and could keep themselves supplied with the relatively perishable caps, most likely the traders who returned to civilization during the winters. The popularity of the plains rifle peaked on the Oregon Trail

Original Hawken rifle taken from the Nez Perce. Note the sparse decoration with brass tacks at the butt. (Courtesy of The Museum of The Fur Trade, Chadron, Nebraska)

during the 1840s and '50s, when most of the former trappers had gone on to other occupations.

So how did the Hawken come to be labeled the mountain man's gun? It said so right on the top flat of the barrels. And this was the time when writers began to romanticize the mountain man. They saw these shaggy old gents lounging around army posts and way stations, leaning on Hawkens; so they soon had the mountaineers swinging Hawkens at Blackfeet in their writings about the rendezvous period.

The Hawken legend might have died with the hyperbole of those times if Thompson/Center had not resurrected the name and pinned it on their modern muzzleloading rifle—at least that's the opinion of John Baird, founder of The National Association of Primitive Riflemen, editor and publisher of *The Buckskin Report*, and author of *Hawken Rifles: The Mountain Man's Choice* and *Fifteen Years in the Hawken Lode*.

"When the T/C Hawken came out, a lot of these gun writers went plowing back through their history books to get some color to throw into their copy," Baird said. "They did a good job of convincing the public that every mountain man across the Missouri River had a Hawken rifle, and that was baloney!"

The Northwest Trade Gun

Let's back up for a minute and take a look at another gun that, whether many mountain men used them or not, was certainly present in substantial numbers during the mountain trade. In the 1700s, English traders began supplying friendly Indians with an inexpensive flintlock musket. As this trade was focused in the Northwest territory, the light musket became known as the Northwest trade gun. Other labels include the London fusil or fusee, Mackinaw gun, and Hudson's Bay fuke.

Actress Victoria Racimo brandishes a Northwest trade gun—a copy of the Indian's beloved London fusil—in a scene from *The Mountain Men*. (Courtesy of Columbia Pictures)

By the time the fur company trappers went into the Rockies, the Northwest gun was a fixture among the Indians. And because the Indians had come to accept certain features as characteristic of the fuke, such as the oversize trigger guard for use with heavy mittens, the brass serpent sideplate, and ribbed brass ramrod thimbles, the Northwest gun changed little until the last batch was peddled from Hudson's Bay Company outposts in the Canadian wilds sometime early in this century.

"White men, too, bought the fusil for use as a hunting gun," writes Charles Hanson in *The Northwest Gun*. "Simplicity and ease of loading made it a favorite of the early buffalo runners. Half-breeds and the more Indian-like trappers used the fusil as their principal gun."

Barrels ranged from thirty to thirty-six inches, but on the plains in the hands of an Indian horseman, a barrel was apt to wind up shorter. With the touchhole of his fuke enlarged slightly, the mounted warrior or hunter could reload in the thick of the chase, frequently turning in an impressive rate of fire. All he needed was a well-knapped flint (something the Indians were no slouches at) set in the jaws of the cock, a mouthful of balls, and a horn of powder.

To reload on the run, he would dump in a load of powder by guess and by gosh (a dangerous practice, to be sure) and spit a ball down after it. The frizzen would already be closed, so when he thumped the buttstock on the ground speeding by below, the ball was seated and priming from the main charge thrown into the pan. There remained only to cock and shoot. No way a rifle, especially a caplock, could compete with the fusil in spraying lead.

Toward the end of the Western Fur Trade Era, the increased firepower of double-barreled arms was tried in the mountains. With the trade caravans, percussion double-barreled shotguns were employed as night-guard guns. And the English double rifle made its debut when the wealthy Scotsman William Drummond Stewart carried a Joseph Manton piece to the rendezvous in 1833. In succeeding years, he reputedly brought more double rifles and distributed them among some of his mountain man friends. (He apparently was not carrying one himself in 1837, as Miller's

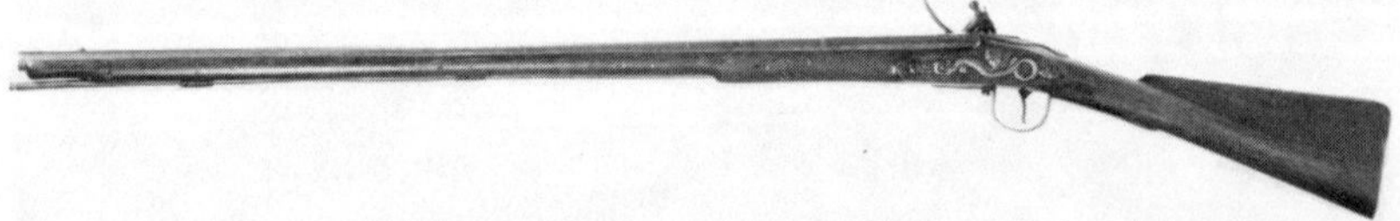

Northwest trade gun, circa 1819, with typical serpent sidelock and oversized trigger guard. (Courtesy of The Museum of The Fur Trade, Chadron, Nebraska)

"English pattern" trade rifle made on military lines by Pennsylvania gunmaker Joseph Henry. These guns were not as popular as the Lancaster-style trade gun, which was basically a Kentucky rifle. (Courtesy of The Museum of The Fur Trade, Chadron, Nebraska)

sketches show him with a long flinter that looks an awful lot like an "English pattern" trade rifle.) Although double rifles were not a common sight at the rendezvous, there can be no doubt that some were there.

Pistols and Cannons

Handguns aren't frequently mentioned in the literature of the fur trade. We know from several accounts that Kit Carson used one in a fracas during the 1835 rendezvous, but there's not a whole lot else to go on. However, Carl P. Russell, in *Firearms, Traps, & Tools of the Mountain Men*, cites a conviction that pistols were a major part of the mountaineer's equipment.

The fast-loading smoothbore horse pistols were probably a favorite, Russell says, and probably in a bore diameter to match the trapper's long arm. That would eliminate the necessity for an extra bullet mold and cleaning jag.

Hanson disagrees slightly. A horse pistol would be a logical choice, he says, but in a much larger bore than the mountaineer's rifle, say .60 or .70 caliber. Hanson also notes the popularity of rifled Kentucky pistols during the era and the eventual presence of the percussion half-stocked plains pistols of the type turned out by J&S Hawken and Henry Deringer (before the latter got into belly guns in a big way).

Revolving handguns—pepperboxes and Colt's Paterson—were around before the end of the Western Fur Trade Era, but I can't find any evidence of their seeing service in the mountains during that time.

At the other end of the scale, there were some cannons around. John Jacob Astor supplied Astoria with four-pounders and apparently abandoned them when the fort was relinquished to the Canadian North West Company at the outset of the War of 1812. In 1824, a party of the Hudson's

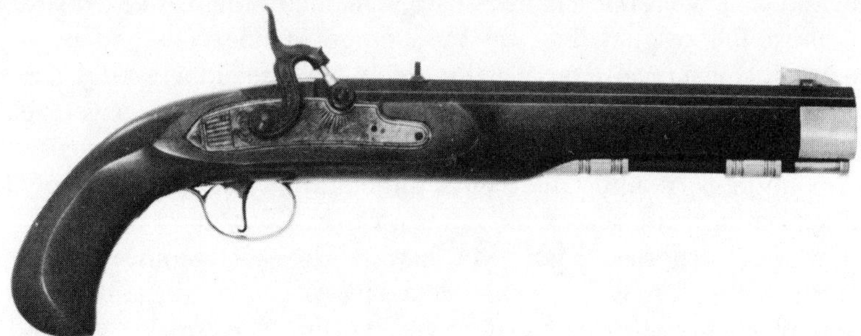

Kentucky pistols were a standard firearm in America during the Western Fur Trade Era. This reproduction is from Connecticut Valley Arms. (Courtesy of Connecticut Valley Arms)

The Lyman Plains Pistol is a good example of the "Hawken-style" handguns which became popular alongside the plains rifle. (Courtesy of Lyman)

Bay Company, which had come out on top in an earlier merger with the North West Company, took a wheeled four-pounder, probably one of Astor's, into the wilderness of what is now Montana. And in 1827, William Ashley broke the trail for hundreds of prairie schooners by dragging a wheeled four-pounder through South Pass. Smaller cannons called swivel guns because of the way they were mounted were commonly found at posts and on keelboats along the Missouri.

Replicas and Reproductions

Now that you have a general idea of what the mountain men used, let's take a look at what buckskinners have available to them. In events where you must follow guidelines set by a group—rendezvous and primitive shoots, for instance—you usually don't have to adhere to what the mountain men actually used, rather you are expected to limit yourself to firearms that were simply in existence in 1840 or before. And usually that means no modern adjustable sights, although internal improvements like coil-spring locks are acceptable in most cases.

The two categories of guns you have to choose from are replicas and reproductions. A replica is a close copy of a specific original gun. I have a replica of a Wheeler-made Northwest trade gun, for example. A reproduction apes the lines and features of a general type of gun. My Kentucky rifle is a reproduction in that it has all the earmarks of that breed of firearm, but it's not a faithful copy of any one particular gun. Replicas are vaunted and usually more expensive; reproductions are fine.

Even a good replica can be expected to need a little doctoring up to *look* right in the hands of a modern mountain man. The muzzleloaders of the mountain men saw some really hard use, and we tend to pamper our guns. One thing that looks out of place on most guns is the finish. Both wood and metal are just a little too slick, a little too polished.

David Higginbotham of League City, Texas, has a ruthless way of dealing with this, with some surprisingly handsome results. He washes the barrel down with muriatic acid (a hydrochloric acid you can buy at builder's supply stores) and puts it aside until a coat of rust builds up. He removes the loose rust with steel wool, rubbing very lightly on the sharp edges of the flats so as not to taken them down to bare metal, then he sets the barrel aside again to rust some more. Finally he rubs it with steel wool once more and "fixes" the browning process with an ammonia bath. Naturally you would want to oil the bore well and plug it securely at both muzzle and nipple port or touchhole before you begin.

Higginbotham takes the finish and the coat of sealer most manufacturers use off the stock with sandpaper. "The only way I can tell you how to do this," he said, "is that once the finish is gone, the sealer looks kinda dull. When you sand through this, the wood looks shiny again. You just have to sand until all the dull is gone." He restains the stock dark and lovingly hand-rubs it with linseed oil.

With the gloss off the wood and a rich, mottled patina on the metal, Higginbotham's guns look like well-preserved originals.

You can also "Indianize" a gun to give it that mountain look. Most Indians and some trappers liked to fancy up their firearms with rows of brass tacks hammered into the stocks. And gun repair in the mountains was usually accomplished with rawhide and sinew. Cracked stocks were mended and barrels even bound to the stocks by stitching on wet rawhide which, when it dried, shrank and bonded like iron bands.

The first time I tried this, I used rawhide from a doe skin. It was too thin and the stitches pulled out. The second time I used rawhide from a steer. It was too thick, wouldn't stretch enough when wet, and therefore didn't bind tight enough when it dried. But on the third try, when I used the shoulder hide off a young whitetail buck, the method worked like a charm. You just have to experiment until you find the right combination of strength and thickness. Incidentally, you can also use this method for keeping your tomahawk head from sliding down its handle, or for binding cracked panels on your knife, or in just about any situation where you would be tempted to use a modern hose clamp.

Other customizing techniques, which may or may not require more gunsmithing talent than you have, include replacing sights and ramrod thimbles. Many 'skinners build their guns the way they want them from kits or parts assembled from hither and yon. Some take their ideas and their checkbooks to custom gunmakers. Most, however, are satisfied with

David "Cripple Creek" Higginbotham browned the barrel of this Trail Guns Armory Tryon with muriatic acid and refinished the stock to make it look like a well-preserved original gun.

production guns right off the shelf or out of the box, and there are some excellent ones available.

Production Guns

The average 'skinner is going to pick a plains rifle and probably one that looks a whole lot like the Hawken of old. While this may still be done because he thinks the Hawken is the only gun "right" for the period, it's more likely because the Hawken or other plains rifle is a damn good gun, short enough of barrel and large enough of bore to be a real hunter.

The Santa Fe Hawken by Allen Fire Arms, the Ithaca/Navy Hawken by Navy Arms, Browning's Jonathan Browning Mountain Rifle, and the Lyman Great Plains Rifle all come pretty close to looking like something turned out by Jake and Sam. To qualify for some primitive shoots, you would have to replace the adjustable sights on the Browning and Great Plains rifle with fixed ones. All come in .54 caliber, which makes them adequate for any game in North America save maybe an irate griz.

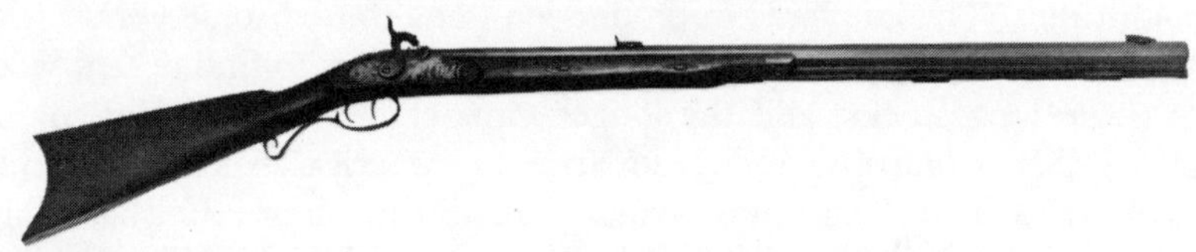

The Lyman Great Plains Rifle is a Hawken look-alike. It combines proper styling with coil-spring dependability. The adjustable rear sight would have to be replaced by a drift-and-file version to meet some primitive shoot standards. (Courtesy of Lyman)

Trail Guns Armory's Mike Powasnick had the discriminating 'skinner in mind when he took a deluxe, engraved original Tryon rifle to Davide Pedersoli Arms in Italy. The result is one of the fanciest replica plains rifles on the market today, and the only one I know of that features the fast, strong back-action lock. Whether any of George Tryon's plains rifles made it to rendezvous or not I have no way of knowing. The Philadelphia gunmaker did supply trade guns during that period, including some pretty good "replicas" of the London fusil. The Tryon from TGA comes in .54 caliber and with fixed sights. A plainer version, also based on Powasnick's original, is sold by Armsport.

The Lyman Trade Rifle, the Connecticut Valley Arms Big Bore (.54 and .58 calibers), and the CVA Mountain Rifle will pass muster as general representations of trade or plains rifles, more so with the addition of some of the custom touches mentioned above.

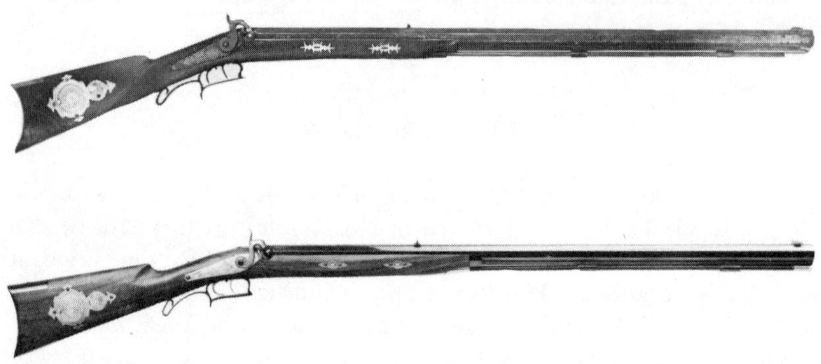

From the original Tryon plains rifle (*top*) sprang the Italian-made replica (*bottom*), marketed by Trail Guns Armory. This new Tryon and a plainer version sold by Armsport are the only modern caplock rifles currently available with the fast, strong back-action lock. (Courtesy of The Trail Guns Armory)

At this writing, you can still arm yourself with a good Kentucky rifle off the shelf, but it appears as though the dean of American firearms is in for tough times. The emphasis in production guns shifted some years ago to the plains type. It's getting harder for manufacturers to find decent wood for those long stocks, and the longer guns create shipping difficulties. CVA, EMF Company, Inc., Euroarms of America, Allen Fire Arms, Navy Arms, and Trail Guns Armory are still marketing finished Kaintucks, and they're still available in kit form from CVA, Hopkins & Allen, and probably others. A good many of the Kentuckies showing up at rendezvous these days are handmade.

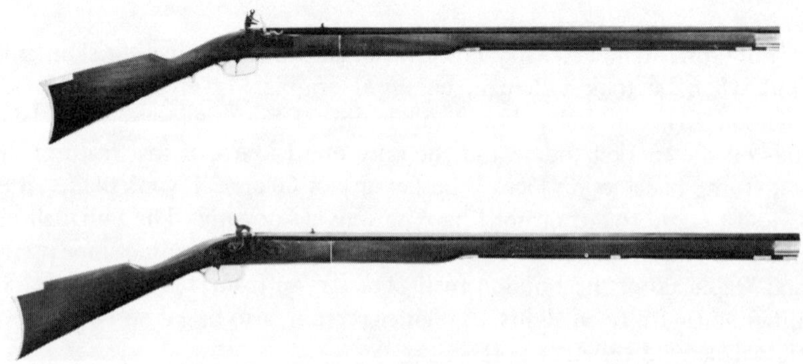

Connecticut Valley Arms' Kentucky rifles feature a two-piece stock, an expediency being forced on the company by the shortage of good wood and shipping difficulties created by long stocks. Other companies are simply dropping long rifles from their lines. (Courtesy of Connecticut Valley Arms)

Dixie Gun Works, the company that started the reproduction landslide with a long rifle from Belgium years ago, is still in the game with an excellent copy of a typical poor boy Kentucky—its Tennessee Mountain Rifle. This .50-caliber long rifle is available in flint *and* percussion (the lock can easily be modified either way), with left-hand and right-hand locks.

The Alamo Long Rifle from Trail Guns Armory. With its classic Roman-nose stock and relatively short barrel, this rifle is reminiscent of a gun on display at the Alamo. (Courtesy of The Trail Guns Armory)

Now if you really want to wow folks at the rendezvous, come packing a replica of the U.S. Rifle Model 1803, the Harper's Ferry rifle field-tested by the Corps of Discovery. Some historians speculate that this was the gun John Colter was toting when he left the expedition to become the first famous mountain man. Replica M1803s, in .58 instead of the original .54 caliber, are sold by Navy Arms and Dixie Gun Works.

Trail Guns Armory is the only source of a percussion double rifle reproducion reminiscent of the Manton double carried by Stewart. But the TGA Kodiak, with its twin adjustable folding-leaf rear sights, wasn't designed for buckskinning. It's a pure hunter. In .58 caliber and loaded with heavy conical bullets, *this* is what you want if you're going to take on Ol' Griz!

Dixie Gun Works sells a Northwest Trade gun made of parts from Curly Gostomski. If you're a do-it-yourselfer, you can obtain the barrel and fixin's directly from him. They come in 24, 20 and 12 gauge and in lengths of thirty, thirty-six and forty-one inches. Write North Star Enterprises, Box 234, Dayton, Ohio 45404.

Some 'skinners opt for a Brown Bess replica (both Dixie and Navy have them) cut down to a buffalo gun and "Indianized."

Dixie, Navy, TGA, and others offer good-quality percussion double-barreled shotguns, in 12 gauge and the potent, goose-getting 10 gauge.

As for handguns, there are plenty of Kentucky pistols around, a few smoothbore dragoon or horse pistols, and several new round-butted Hawken or plains pistols. Most mountain rendezvous, which cut off progress at 1840 or thereabouts, will allow the use of replica Colt Paterson cap-and-ball revolvers. Patersons may have been in circulation as early as 1836, and Kit Carson was reportedly packing one by 1841. Paterson replicas are sold by Navy Arms and Allen Fire Arms. Pepperboxes, which were the most common repeaters during the mountain man's time and are

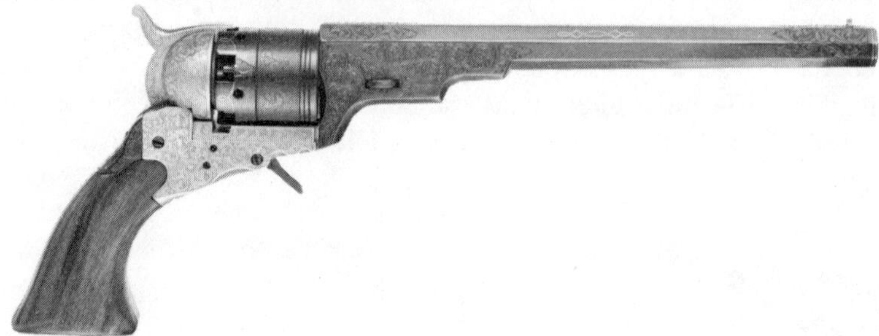

Because they're expensive to make and demand is slight, replica Patersons may soon be nearly as rare as the originals. Navy Arms and Allen Fire Arms are two companies still offering them. This one is a Navy. (Courtesy of Navy Arms)

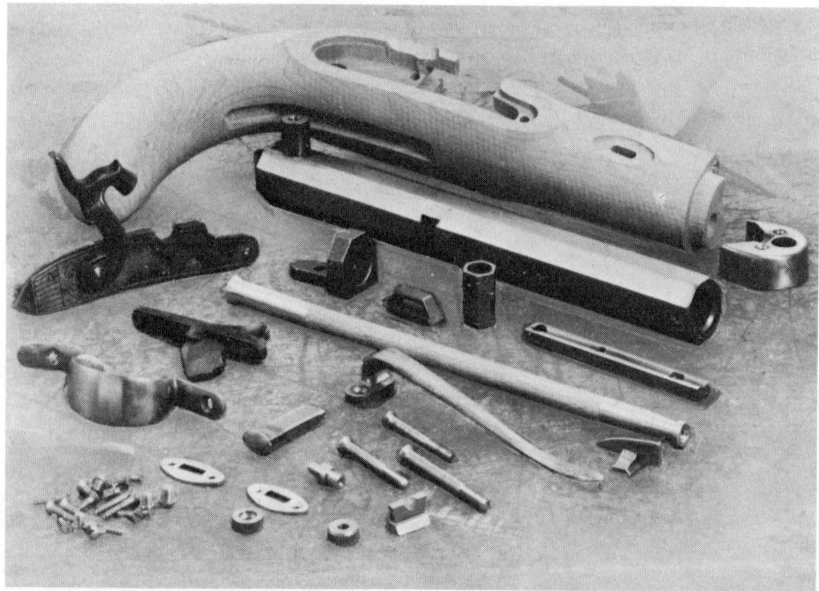

Inexpensive kits, like this one for a mountain pistol from Connecticut Valley Arms, are a way to save money and add to your muzzleloading arsenal. (Courtesy of Connecticut Valley Arms)

certainly more common than the Patersons as reproductions today, just don't seem to make it at the rendezvous. Maybe they speak to us more of riverboats and silk shirts than of the mountains and buckskins.

Just as it was for the old trappers, a black-powder pistol is a worthy companion to the 'skinner's long gun. More of the combat-style shooting events like the mountain man run are incorporating the use of handguns. The thoughtful muzzleloading hunter should pack a pistol, when it's legal, for that merciful *coup de grace*. And tucked in your belt or sash, a pistol becomes an effective piece of costuming.

Authentic but Practical

When it comes to selecting any of the guns, but particularly the long arms, you really need to think beyond the historical and, if you'll pardon the expression, the theatrical considerations. Hunting and primitive matches are a big chunk of the fun in buckskinning, and you'll want a gun that not only looks right, but performs well.

Take rifles—you need a gun that will shoot patched round balls because that's what the mountain men used. The Minie-ball, the first really workable long bullet, didn't come onto the scene until about 1840, and that was in France.

It would take an expert like John Wootters or Walt Viggers to fully explain it, but basically the ability of a rifle to handle round balls is a function of its rifling: It must have a fairly slow twist, something like one

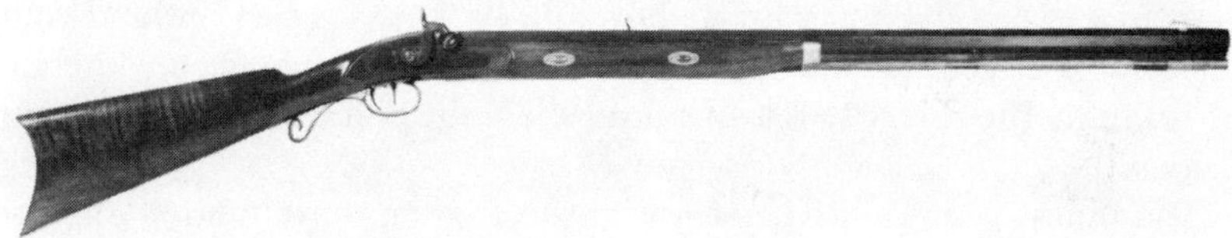

The Ithaca-Navy Hawken, an excellent copy of the type of rifle turned out by Sam and Jake Hawken of St. Louis, comes in .54 caliber, with a 1-in-66 twist. It would be a good choice for a round ball hunting rifle. (Courtesy of Navy Arms)

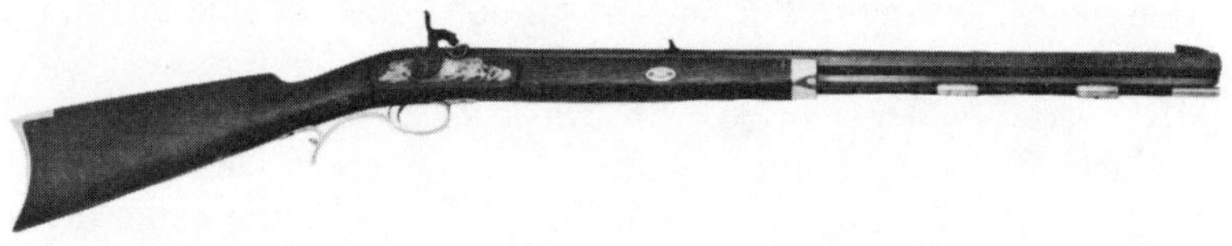

A general reproduction of the Indian rifles turned out for the fur trade, the Lyman Rifle combines authenticity, including a fixed sight, with the 1-in-48 twist needed to shoot Maxi-balls and other modern conicals. (Courtesy of Lyman)

full rotation of the ball over a lateral distance of sixty-six inches, and fairly deep grooves, about ten thousands of an inch. These figures are like the EPA mileage estimates, to use for comparison. The modern muzzleloaders that are manufactured primarily with conical bullets in mind typically have one twist in forty-eight inches and rifling as shallow as three thousands of an inch.

Personally, I wouldn't hunt whitetail with anything less than a .50 caliber. People take them with .45s all the time, I know, but I can't recommend it. A .45 or a .36 is adequate for small game and great fun for plinking, but in my view they ought to be second guns. Even if you've never done any deer hunting, as a 'skinner you'll probably start.

For elk or moose, you need at least a .54 caliber. And when you start talking grizzly bears, I quit talking round balls. Give me a .58 with at least 500 grains of conical bullet. Or better yet, two of them.

If you're a newcomer to the muzzleloading sport, or if you're just going to own one gun, I suggest you make it a caplock. A good, well-tuned flintlock in the hands of an expert is as fast, sometimes faster, than a percussion. But they're temperamental and require almost constant adjusting. I'm not saying a flintlock has no place on a serious hunting gun; Pennsylvania won't let you take advantage of the state's special muzzleloading provisions for hunters unless you shoot one. But you should know what you're getting into.

The warning about flinters goes double for fowling pieces. It's one thing to sit in a tree in the rain with a tallow-and-beeswax "gasket" around your pan to protect your priming until you can take that one shot at a whitetail. It's quite another to try to reload a flintlock in the rain while teal buzz your decoys.

And unless you're a crackerjack wingshot, serious bird hunting calls for at least a 12 gauge.

Again, if you want to handicap yourself in the name of sport, authenticity, or whatever—as I often do with my 20-gauge fusil—at least do it with your eyes open.

I don't consider any of the muzzleloading pistols suitable for hunting deer. And you should be aware that while the federal government doesn't classify black-powder guns as firearms, most states do. Handguns, particularly, can get you into trouble in a hurry; check your local laws.

By far the most important consideration when selecting a muzzleloading gun—in spite of all that I've said—is to choose one that *feels* right. That could mean how it feels in the crook of your arm, or how it looks propped in the corner, or what visions of the past it stirs in your mind. That gun is your passport to another era. It'll be your frequent companion. It'll develop a personality of its own.

And it may release a long-imprisoned side of *you*, too.

5

Pouches and Powder Horns

Having properly armed yourself as a mountain man, your next task, almost as much fun, is to equip yourself with the proper gear for the care and feeding of a muzzleloading gun—and to do it without the modern conveniences of the shirtsleeve muzzleloader. No Pyrodex, Poly-Patches, and Speed Shells for you, friend!

The first thing you need is something nice and primitive to carry all your primitive tackle in and about. Customarily, that's a bag with a shoulder strap called a hunting pouch or, more frequently these days, a "shooting bag" or "possibles bag."

Personally, I don't like the term "possibles bag" because in the nineteenth century that referred to a second satchel hung over the opposite shoulder or from the horn of a saddle, to be used as sort of a suitcase. In the writings that have come down from the early days, the hunting pouch is more commonly called a "bullet pouch" or "shot pouch," although it usually contained more than just balls or shot.

It's a small matter; you may call it what you want. I would hope that you don't call it what my wife does: "What's that you're making there, dear? Another *purse?*"

In design and function, though, the hunting pouch resembles nothing so much as a ladies' shoulder bag. In fact, I have a hunting buddy who actually uses a purse, discarded by a girl friend. Others, equally unconcerned with authenticity, use army surplus gas mask bags and even camera bags. They find the ancient form of the hunting pouch hard to beat.

It may well be that some form of bag suspended from a shoulder strap has been around as long as the most basic clothing. It stands to reason that man had to become a hunter before he could be much of a clotheshorse, since he needed to slay the animals to get their hides. And he needed weaponry before he could be much of a hunter. So where did he carry the day's supply of rocks, spear points, or whatever? Much as we take them for

The author frequently carries his shooting supplies in a primitive hunting pouch even when he's hunting in modern garb. The pouch and horn, like the muzzleloading rifle, add a certain *feel* to hunting that is pleasurable. (Photo by Larry Bozka)

granted, pockets are a relatively recent fashion. Certainly the caveman's hairy tunic didn't have any.

By the time of the mountain rendezvous, the method of carrying ammunition and gun tools had pretty much been standardized as described in a note by the artist Alfred Jacob Miller with his sketch of a "typical" trapper: "Over his left shoulder and under his right arm hung his buffalo powderhorn, a bullet pouch in which he carries balls, flint, and steel, with other knick-knacks."

Whether or not it had a complete carrying strap of its own, the powder horn was usually attached to the strap of the pouch so that the two hung together at the rifleman's side, with the horn normally suspended near the center of the bag.

Types of Pouches

Basic form aside, there are differences in the design and decoration of both pouches and horns that deserve attention. Many of the differences are subtle, and there are some styles that would put you anywhere from

A typical Rocky Mountain trapper, sketched by Alfred Jacob Miller, carried his buffalo powderhorn and hunting pouch (commonly called a bullet pouch) over his left shoulder and under his right arm. (Courtesy of The Thomas Gilcrease Institute of American History and Art, Tulsa, Oklahoma)

seventeenth-century Virginia to the Civil War period and beyond. Before you buy or make a pouch-and-horn set, you would do well to look at *The Kentucky Rifle Hunting Pouch* by Madison Grant. The book contains nearly 150 photos of original pouches and horns spanning more than 100 years. There's also a happy sprinkling of knives, bullet molds, shot bags, and other original shooting implements pictured. Many of the mail-order houses catering to buckskinners carry Grant's book.

Most hunting pouches were made of leather, which is durable and was easily obtained. Sailcloth or canvas was probably the next most popular material, especially with the military—and there's a lot to be said for it. My favorite pouch is one I stitched out of white cotton duck, dyed with tea, and waterproofed with (dare I say it?) a commercial preparation out of a spray can. I like the looks of my heavy leather "mountain bag" better, but the canvas pouch is lighter and easier to get stuff in and out of, and the cloth clings in place at my side a whole lot better than does the slick leather of the other pouch.

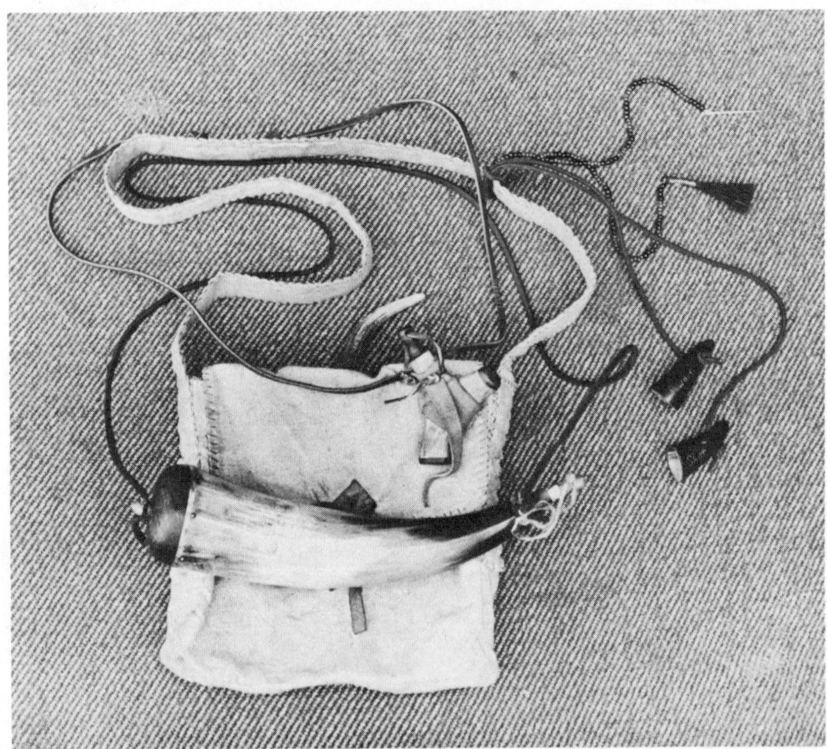

Light canvas hunting pouch favored by the author. The vent pick and brush set is handmade using a hank of horsehair and a common sewing needle. The section of antler above the horn contains priming powder.

In *The Kentucky Rifle Hunting Pouch*, Grant identifies four basic shapes of pouches: the D shape, which is the most common; the heart shape; the square shape; and the commodious kidney shape (Figure 5-1). The flap usually matches the shape of the pouch or is semicircular, but other variations are found, including the V-shaped and the "beaver-tail" flaps

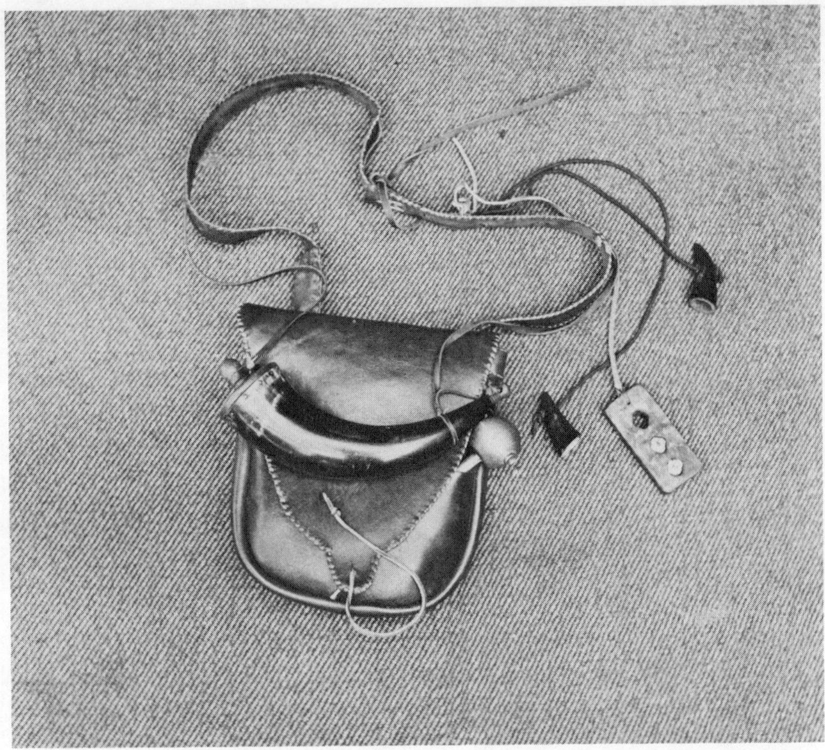

Author's heavy leather "mountain" bag. A bullet block and powder measures for two different guns are hung within easy reach.

popular during the time of the mountain men. According to Grant, double pouches—two superimposed compartments—can be found in any of the basic shapes. They were more popular in the East than with the mountain men.

Not all mountain men made their own pouches, nor should you feel you have to. Some traded for Indian-made bags or obtained commercially made bags from traders. So don't feel guilty about buying one off a rendezvous trade blanket, at a muzzleloading shop, or from a mail-order house.

Hunting pouches weren't machine-stitched until about 1840, the year of the last mountain rendezvous. The die-hard 'skinner wouldn't be caught dead with a machine-stitched pouch, but no one is going to boot you out of camp for toting one. It's strictly a matter of conscience.

Some pouches, particularly those made by Indian women, were fringed and decorated with quillwork or the large pony beads in basic colors and simple designs. (The intricate work with the smaller seed beads came a

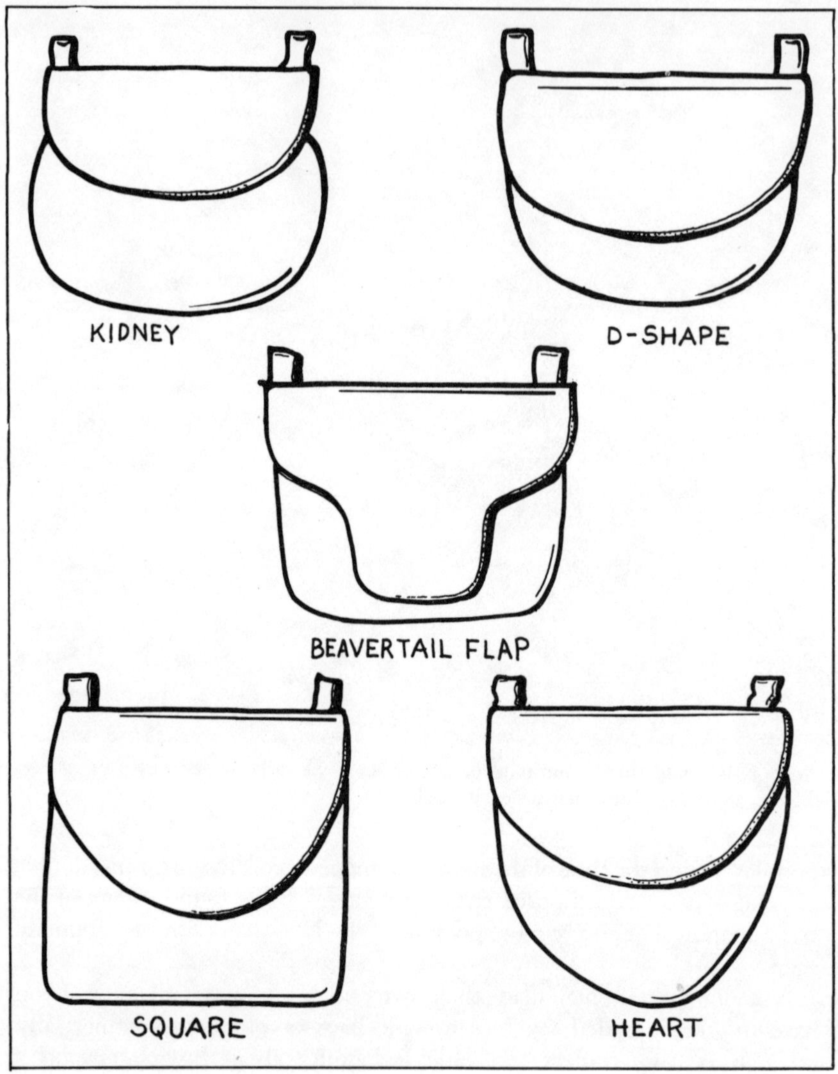

FIGURE 5–1   Basic shapes of hunting pouches.

decade or more later.) You wouldn't have to surrender such a pouch to the dog soldiers, but when a primitive event cuts off progress at 1840 or thereabouts, it's bad manners to knowingly wear or carry something that wasn't around yet. What it does is cheapen the efforts of those who are trying to preserve those years by being historically correct. And 1860s beadwork, unlike machine stitching, really stands out to the initiated.

Other authentic decorations include tooling or stamped designs (common on commercial pouches), fur coverings, and borders and appliqued designs of trade cloth or wool.

Powder Horns

You may be surprised to learn that some, maybe many, mountain men bought commercially-made powder horns made in the eastern states or imported from Europe. The powder horn, along with the moccasin and coonskin hat, has come to represent the epitome of frontier improvisation. But in truth the powder horn was more than just a conveniently available container: It was and is a nearly ideal container for packing around black powder. It's tough yet lightweight, water resistant, impervious to sunlight, and its shape fits the contours of the body or hunting pouch. In frontier America, it also happened to be convenient.

That didn't mean the only way to get a powder horn was to cut one off a buffalo and whittle a plug for it. Makers of guns for the fur trade like Leman and Tryon supplied finished powder horns, and horns continued to come in from Europe, to supply both the trapper and Indian with a smooth, ready-to-fill powder container. Charles Hanson reports in *The Museum of the Fur Trade Quarterly*, that the American Fur Company sold "3½ doz. powder horns @ $7.50" to William H. Ashley in St. Louis in 1823.

The powder horn as an expression of individual frontier art, like the sailor's scrimshaw, did exist, of course. It reached its zenith in the eighteenth century when, as companions to the delicate Kentucky rifles, the horns were elaborately worked and etched with maps, figures, dates, battle scenes, and inscriptions; such as "John Q. Leatherstocking, His Horn" and "I Powder, with Brother Ball, Hero-like Do Conquer All." Not all eighteenth-century horns were fancied up, by any means. But those that were tended to be pretty fancy.

While the horns of the nineteenth century were less likely to be elaborately carved and etched, their construction—especially of the commercial ones—became more sophisticated, featuring fancy turned or carved plugs, perhaps inset with mirrors or furnished with carved or cast finials in place of the crude staples or wooden knobs found on earlier horns. Some were even fitted with spouts that threw a measured charge, like those found on flasks.

Today you can buy a plain-vanilla powder horn for about what one cost General Ashley wholesale. Kits are even cheaper, naturally, and it's no great trick to make one yourself out of a shed cowhorn you find in the pasture.

To attach your horn to your pouch, hang the two together from a limb or something and securely (but temporarily) tie the two carrying straps together about midway down the front and the back, as they would be on your body. Then slip them on to see if the ties allow you enough slack in the horn strap to go through the motions of unstopping the horn, filling your powder measure, and corking it back up again—all without tugging unduly at your pouch. If you don't have enough freedom of movement, you may want to move the ties upward. Or if your horn has too much swing to it and won't ride securely on your pouch, you may want to move them down. When you find the right spots to anchor the horn's strap to that of the pouch, you can make them fast by cutting slits in the wider pouch strap and threading the other through, or by sewing or tying them together, or by snipping the horn strap and tying the loose ends at the points you've established.

A priming horn is hung in the same manner, usually just above the big horn.

Stuff to Have Handy

As in the old days, many 'skinners like to carry small, razor-sharp patch knives somewhere on the outside of their pouches where they are handy, yet not likely to snag on something. The most common methods are to fasten a small sheath on the strap so that the knife is positioned near the wearer's chest, and to attach the sheath behind the pouch so the handle of the knife protrudes just above the roll of the flap.

The well-appointed pouch-and-horn outfit will also have some other gear hanging externally: a nipple pick or vent pick and pan brush; powder measure; a bullet block holding prepatched round balls; short starter; and maybe some means of carrying and dispensing caps. These are the items routinely needed for every shot and it's nice to be able to get to them without digging around in your pouch.

An authentic capper is easy to make with a small piece of thick leather such as the stuff they call "live oak." Cut the leather into whatever shape pleases you (a simple disk is most common but I've seen arrowheads, bear tracks, and others) and punch a line of holes around the edge, each just large enough to hold a No. 11 percussion cap securely. Add a thong to attach it to your pouch, or hang it around your neck, and you're ready to go. Just place a cap on the nipple and peel away the leather capper.

I've heard tell of priming horns being used to carry caps. The hole would be just large enough to allow one cap at a time to pass through. I can see how that would be a natural adaptation of existing equipment as the owner went from a flintlock to a percussion. I can also see how such an arrangement could be pretty impractical. The caps would rattle around inside the horn, for one thing. And you would have to be dexterous enough to shake out only *one* cap. (Bullets come out of a machine gun one

Bullet block, short starter, and leather capper (hanging below shirt) can all be easily reached by this buckskin-clad rifleman. Notice that the short starter has a hole drilled through it and a lanyard attached.

at a time, you know.) Finally, you would wind up with a cap in your hand, and those little items are notoriously hard to hold onto when it's cold, or in the excitement of a hunt.

There's a replica of a nineteenth-century mechanical capper on the market which comes in brass or German silver. It's made by Tedd Cash of Waunakee, Wisconsin. I have a brass one that has mellowed to an olive-gold patina and I use it whether I'm hunting in buckskins or L.L. Bean chic. It works fine and holds a whole bunch of caps.

You can buy a finished bullet block, but they are easily made at home. Just take a piece of hardwood that's roughly as thick as the diameter of the balls you'll be carrying in it, and cut it to whatever shape and size you like. A rectangle with one or two rows of holes is probably the most functional.

For a .45-caliber gun, drill your holes with a $^{29}\!/_{64}$-inch bit. A .50 caliber requires a half-inch bit. And a .54 needs a $^{35}\!/_{64}$-inch bit. Not everyone has the odd-ball sizes, and not every hardware store can furnish you with them, either. You can drill holes for a .45 caliber with a $^{7}\!/_{16}$-inch bit and ream them out with a rattail file. Holes drilled with a $^{9}\!/_{16}$-inch bit will be a little loose, but may serve depending upon the actual diameter of your ball and the thickness of your pouch.

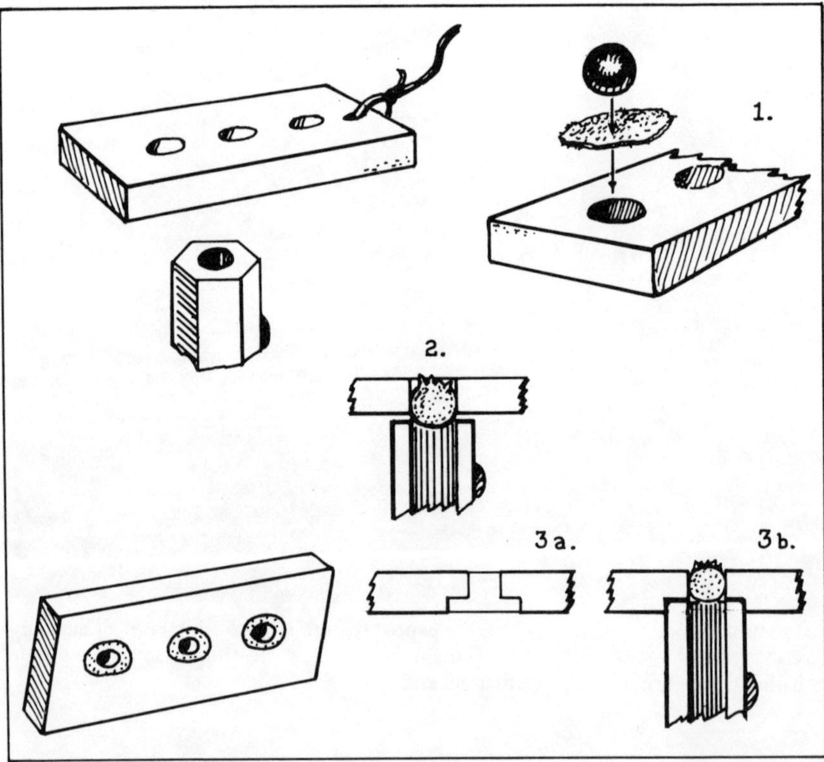

FIGURE 5–2   Loading a bullet block: 1. Load with prelubricated patches; 2. push the ball through the hole just enough so that it can be lined up by "feeling" it in the muzzle. Alternatively, 3a. a larger recess can be drilled in the block so it fits over the muzzle when 3b. positioning the ball.

To load a bullet block (Figure 5-2), place a piece of greased patching over the hole and push a ball into *and slightly through* the hole. The convex surface of the patched ball extending beyond the bottom of the block gives you a tactile guide for lining up the block with the muzzle of your gun (that is, you will be able to feel the ball corralled within the bore). With the ball in place in the block, trim the excess patching flush with the top of the block.

When you're ready to load your gun, simply align the patched ball with the bore, poke it down with your short starter, and follow up with your ramrod.

Some bullet blocks are made a little thicker than the diameter of the ball, and in the bottom of the block you overlap each hole with a countersunk one that is large enough to accommodate the whole muzzle of the rifle. You fit it over the muzzle and the ball is automatically lined up with the bore (Figure 5-2, 3b).

If you do a lot of stump shooting and whatnot at rendezvous, you might want a bullet block that will carry as many as a dozen balls. The only time I load out of a block is when I'm hunting, so I'm happy with one that measures two-by-four inches and holds three .50-caliber balls.

A powder measure dangling from your pouch provides a real shortcut over having to fish out an adjustable measure. True-to-the-period measures can be fashioned from horn or hollowed-out antler tips, bone, or wood. Pour a premeasured charge into the cavity, mark the level, and cut your backwoods measure flush with the mark. Some of the old homemade measures had a scoop-shaped portion left remaining above the level mark to help direct the loose powder down the bore.

If there's enough solid material beneath the hollow portion of the measure, you can drill a hole through for its thong. Otherwise, cut a groove around it to hold the thong in place.

A flintlock shooter will just about always have a vent pick and brush dangling from his pouch strap. The pick is needed to clear the touchhole between shots; if grains of powder from the main charge clog the hole, the spark has to burn though as with a fuse and the result is a delayed ignition. The brush is used to "unload" a flinter by dusting priming powder out of the pan. Replica pick-and-brush combinations are inexpensive. Or you can make one, as I did, by stringing a big sewing needle and a hank of horsehair together with artificial sinew.

Caplock shooters shouldn't overlook the nipple pick. Fired caps often leave big flakes of residue that block the channel to the charge. They break up easily under the pick.

The other item you should consider holstering outside the confines of your hunting pouch is your short starter. The most common type of short starter is a wooden ball with about five inches of dowel sticking out of it. The dowel is tipped with a brass cap which is concave to keep it from slipping off the ball. Another concave brass piece protrudes a fraction of an inch from the ball at a right angle to the dowel. You use the short brass piece to start your patched round ball in the bore of your gun, then the dowel to push it far enough down to make room for your ramrod. With a bullet block, however, you use only the dowel.

Some 'skinners like to make fancy short starters out of antler or bone. Dixie Gun Works sells a short starter kit for a couple of bucks that includes the ball, dowel, and brass caps. You can throw away the wooden ball and use the other parts with your piece of antler or whatever if you want to get fancy.

Stuff to Put Inside

With so much hanging outside your pouch, you may wonder what on earth is left to put inside. Plenty, believe me. Here, I have the pouch I use with my .50-caliber percussion rifle handy. Let's just go through it and see what we find:

Short starter and bullet block, with a thong for attaching the block to the hunting pouch. The short starter is usually carried on the pouch strap, tucked into the shooter's belt, or otherwise kept handy. (Photo by John Wootters)

Roll of patching, tied with yarn. This is a good grade of pillow ticking sold by J.C. Penney's. After much washing to remove the sizing, it mikes out at nineteenth-thousandths inch. I tear it into strips about an inch wide and walk around at the range with one hanging out of my mouth. That way one end is always spit-lubricated for the next shot. (My patches for hunting are lubricated with beeswax, however. I used to use beeswax and tallow, but it gets too hot down here in Texas and that combination tended to run. Now I carry beeswax in my patchbox like the old-timers did. All I have to do is open the cover, rub the patching in the cavity and it's lubricated.)

Bundle of precut cleaning patches. I use army surplus .50-caliber cleaning patches. If before you leave the range or the field, you idly run a half-dozen spit patches through, alternating them with dry ones, you won't have a heck of a lot to do when you get around to boiling some water.

Small corked vial of alcohol for cleaning oil from the bore before the first loading.

Tin of extra caps.

Leather pouch of balls.

Hollowed-out piece of antler containing FFFFg (priming powder) in case a damp charge needs help. You remove the nipple, pour in a few grains, replace the nipple and recap, and she'll just about always go.

Nipple wrench, for when a charge gets damp.

Small disk of heavy leather to keep the charge from getting damp. It's not smart to keep your gun capped in camp. You place the leather disk over the bare nipple, lower the hammer on it, and that effectively seals it.

Extra nipple.

Cleaning jag.

Corkscrew-like patch worm for when the cleaning patches slip off the jag way down the barrel.

Ball puller (a screw that attaches to the end of the ramrod same as the jag) in case a charge simply won't go off, or maybe wasn't dumped down there in the first place.

Small corked vial of gun oil.

Hand-forged screwdriver.

Leather pouch containing firesteel and flint.

Old musket-cap tin containing charcloth and tinder. I found that rubbing beeswax around the outside rim helps waterproof the container.

Replica of nineteenth-century compass with sundial. Doesn't tell time worth a darn, nor will it give you your directions by degrees, but it will point which way to fetch yourself.

Snakebite kit. Not the least bit authentic, but nice to have in Texas, and other places.

Just about the same things are in the canvas pouch I use with my flintlocks, without the obvious items like the nipple wrench, and with the addition of extra flints, extra pieces of leather used for holding flints in the jaws of the cock, and a hand-forged flint-knapper (the same tool I call a screwdriver when it's in the other pouch).

Homemade wads and a bag of shot may replace the patching and balls if I'm carrying my trade gun. The wads are made of toilet paper (I use pre-1840 white) from a recipe given by Mike "Two Bears" Hughes. You take a cheap cutting board, about three quarters of an inch thick, and drill it full of holes. Use a ⅝-inch bit for a 20 gauge and ²³⁄₃₂ bit for 12 gauge. Felt wads and cardboard over-shot cards are relatively easy to find for a 12 gauge, however.

A Do-It-Yourself Pouch

If you've been getting along with a store-bought pouch, you'll probably find making your own a worthwhile project. It's not that difficult, and you get to put pockets and partitions where *you* want them. But, as the above

Michael "Two Bears" Hughes' recipe for making shotgun wads: Secure a board with holes in it to one without holes and pack the cavities tightly with wet toilet paper. When the wads dry, pop them out and break a small piece off one end of each. You have a thick over-powder wad and a thin one for over the shot.

list (just the basics, really) of what goes inside the pouch suggests, you had better make it big.

The design stage is by far the most critical. You must figure out the dimensions of each piece accurately enough so they join where they should and form the final product you had in mind. A pattern on butcher paper or grocery sacks is a good start, but before you start carving up expensive leather, I suggest you actually stitch together a prototype of oilcloth or canvas. That way you can test your theories about partitions and such, and you can find out if the pouch will actually hold all your junk.

First select a basic shape and draw it full-size on paper as though the pouch were lying on its back and the flap were open (Figure 5-3). What you're drawing, in other words, is the main piece that forms the back and flap. Now draw a straight line, using a ruler or other straight edge, smack down the middle of your pattern, top to bottom. Cut out one of the halves.

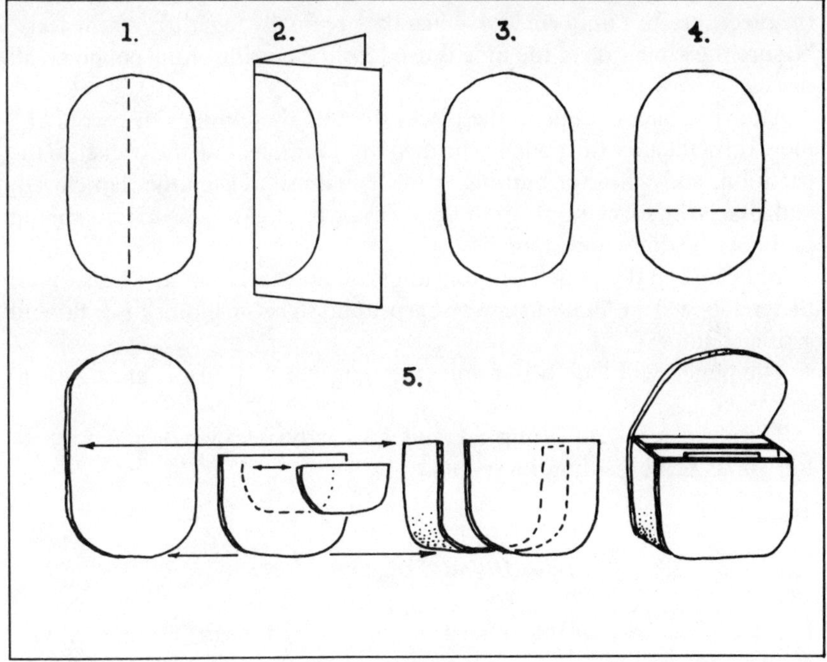

FIGURE 5–3 Making a pattern for a hunting pouch: 1. Sketch the shape and size as though the pouch were lying on its back with the flap open, then cut out the pattern and cut it in half; 2. transfer the half-pattern to another piece of paper that is folded in half; 3. cut this out and open to give a symmetrical pattern; 4. use the bottom third or so (depending on how high the pouch will be) to create a pattern for the front and any partitions and 5. cut a rectangular strip to separate the front and back sections. The width of this strip determines the depth of the pouch.

Take another piece of paper and fold it in half. Transfer your cut out pattern-half to the second piece of paper by aligning the straight edge with the fold and tracing around the rest. Cut out the new pattern and unfold, like a paper doll. With this extra step you're sure of getting a symmetrical version of the original shape you drew freehand.

You will need to duplicate the bottom half or a little less of your new pattern. This piece will be the front of the pouch. And you need a rectangular piece that is as long as the sides and bottom of the pouch and as wide as you want the pouch to be thick. Finally, you need patterns for, let's say, one partition (essentially the same as the front piece or maybe a little shorter), a pocket, and the carrying strap.

Remember, there must be enough flap to cover the opening of the pouch and overlap the front to where it fastens.

When you're ready to make your leather pouch, lay all the patterns out on the hide at once. You can make the most efficient use of the expensive leather that way, and you can better match up grain or texture, so that all the pieces create a uniform look when they're finally together. At the least, be sure the same side of the hide is used for the outside of the pouch on all pieces.

After you have cut out all the pieces, first do those things that would be more difficult after the pouch is formed; for example, sew the pocket to the partition, add whatever buttons or ties you'll use to keep the flap closed, and attach the carrying strap to the sides or back. Any decoration should probably be done now, too.

You can lace the pouch by punching the holes with an awl first, but a better job will be done using a sharp upholstery or glover's needle and artificial sinew.

The pouch will look better and be stronger if you turn it inside-out to sew it.

The above is just an example; coming up with your own design is what's fun about making a hunting pouch.

Making a Powder Horn

Powder horns are available in kit form, or you can start from scratch with an old horn you find lying in the pasture.

If your discarded cowhorn has a core to it, remove it by boiling. This is a pretty smelly process, best done outside and downwind. The boiling also softens the horn and makes it easier to work. You've probably seen one of these little, flat priming flasks made of horn; it's shaped by boiling the horn until it becomes soft, then holding it in a vice or under weights until it dries and hardens.

The inside of the horn may need a little smoothing with sandpaper, but the real work comes in paring down the rough exterior. You file it or scrape it with a length of old hacksaw blade or even a piece of glass—whatever works best for you. Finish up with fine sandpaper or a cloth buffing wheel.

Now's the time to do the basic shaping of the horn. Filing flat panels around the tip of the horn is a popular embellishment, for example. And you'll need to cut a groove around the horn near the tip for the attachment of the carrying strap.

Measure the interior of the horn from its opening to where the cavity stops and solid horn begins. You can use a broom straw or something similar, marking the distance with your thumb, since the measurement isn't critical. You simply want to make sure you leave at least a half-inch of solid horn when you cut off the tip.

After cutting the tip, or the point, into a smooth, flat face, cut the large end to smooth it and provide a uniform opening to accept the plug (Figure 5-4).

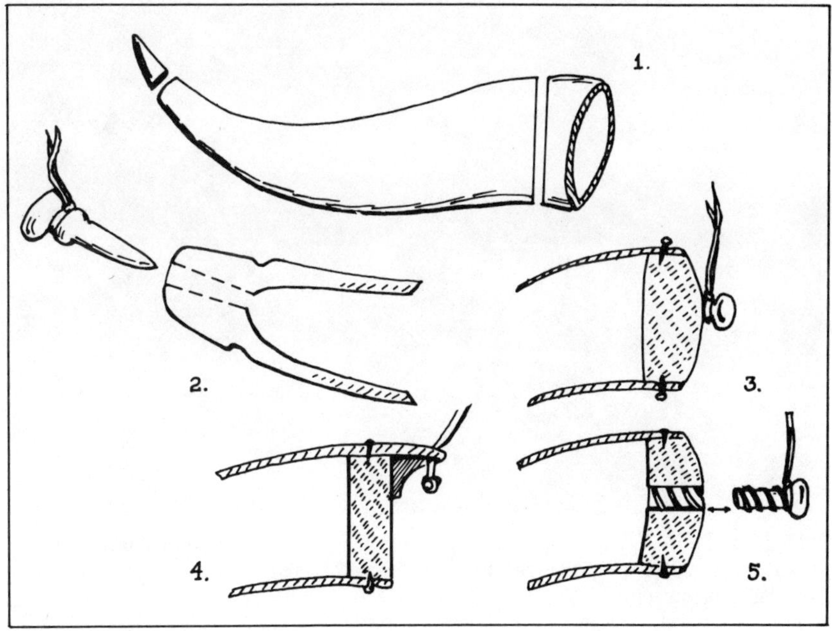

FIGURE 5–4 Steps in making a powder horn: 1. Trim the ends; 2. drill the tip and carve a wooden stopper to fit; 3. shape and install a block of wood to plug the large opening, first carving or attaching a finial for attaching the carrying strap. Alternative ways of attaching a carrying strap are shown in 4. and 5.

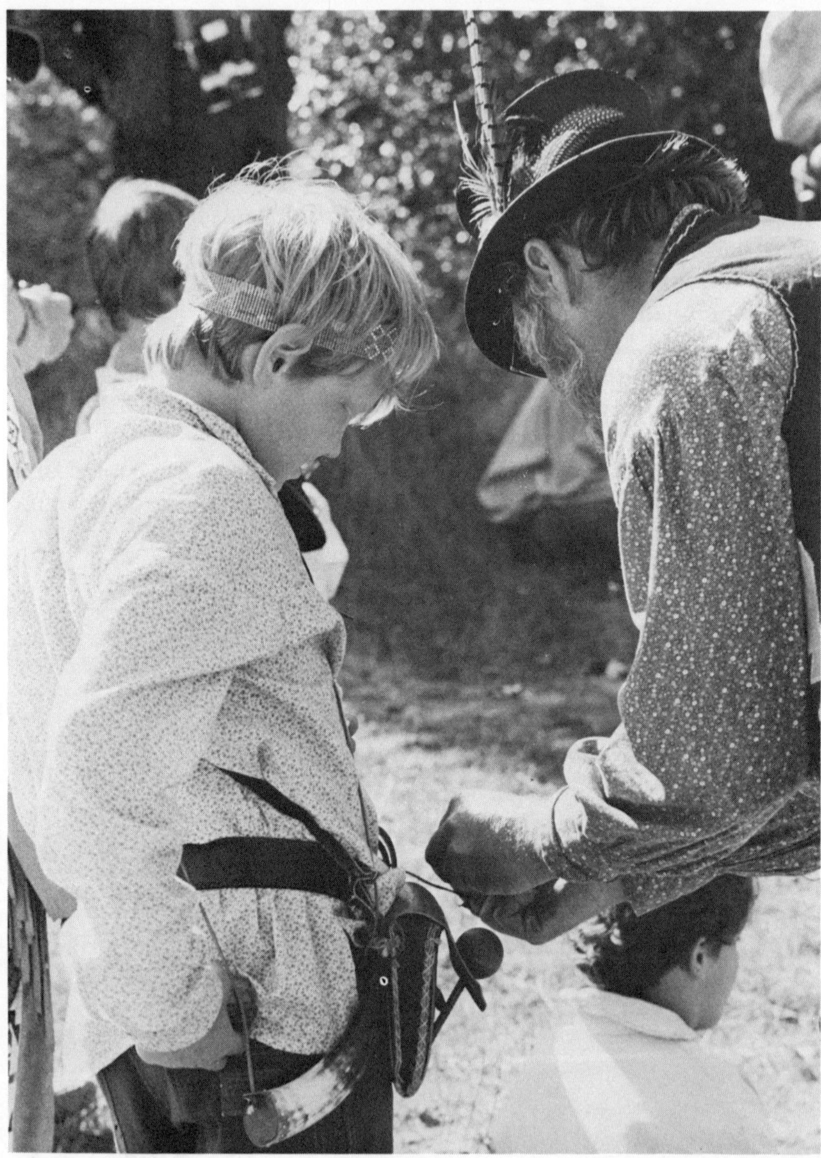

"Dad, can I borrow a few caps?" Once he gets resupplied, this young 'skinner will be ready to go with his lightweight pouch and horn. Note how the horn is attached to the carrying strap.

Drill a ⁵⁄₁₆-inch hole in the face of the tip if you're going to be using the horn for your main powder supply; ¼-inch for priming horns. Ream the hole out just a bit at the outer end, then you'll be ready to carve a wooden stopper for it.

To plug up the large opening, shape a block of wood so that it will fit snugly inside and look pleasing on the outside. Some folks use a relatively soft wood like white pine for the actual plug, then glue a more attractive piece on the end where it shows. The circumference of the plug should be smooth, but it doesn't necessarily have to match the shape of the horn's opening exactly. Hold the large end of the horn in boiling water and it will become soft enough to conform to the shape of the plug. You can improve the seal a little by coating the plug with beeswax before inserting it in the horn, but the fit must be fairly snug to begin with. Secure it with nails or brass tacks.

A knob, or finial, in the middle of the plug is a popular way to attach the carrying strap, although many original horns had nails or staples for the purpose. The finial can be carved from the plug itself or fashioned from an ornamental attachment like an antique drawer knob, bear claw, or anything else your imagination and desire for authenticity can create.

One handy variation is to use a removable finial that is threaded or knurled (you can buy brass ones) so that you can remove it and use the opening for filling your horn. It takes doggone-near all day to pour a half-pound of FFg through a ⁵⁄₁₆-inch hole, I can tell you.

Another way to attach the carrying strap to the large end of the horn is to leave a portion protruding beyond the plug and drill holes in it.

The decorative etching nowadays called "scrimshaw," after the carving done by sailors on ivory and bone, can be done with the inexpensive woodcarving tools sold in hobby shops. Crude designs can be layed out in grease pencil and the grease burnished off after the design is cut. For finer work, paint the horn with white tempera and do your drawing with a hard lead pencil. The water-based tempera will wash right off. To make the finished etching stand out, brush in a waterproof ink and polish off the excess.

To the buckskinner as it was to the mountain man, a horn container is useful for more than carrying black powder. They make great primitive containers for salt and pepper, corn meal, flour, and sugar.

And a nicely finished horn, secured to its companion hunting pouch, is a handsome thing to have hanging beneath your gun between hunts and rendezvous.

6

Tomahawks and Knives

As buckskinners, you and I aren't likely to be bushwacked by more Blackfeet than we have bullets seated over dry powder. Nor is it likely we'll be chewed by a grizzly for failing to knap our flints.

We don't need knives and tomahawks as weapons anymore, thank goodness, but we still need them for chopping firewood, dressing deer, trimming patches, and separating a good cheekful of tobacco from the rest of the twist.

From the earliest times, America's backwoodsmen amused themselves by throwing knives and tomahawks, and at gatherings before, during, and after the rendezvous period they held contests of their skills. (It was a game even then; as weapons, tomahawks, and knives were used to hack and slash.)

Today, most buckskinners' events feature knife and tomahawk throws. Some, like the mountain man run and all its variations, incorporate skill with edged weapons alongside the use of firearms in mountain-style war games.

And knives are a major part of a 'skinner's costume. In fact, the big flashy fighting knives are of use for little else.

Bowies and Other Fighters

By far the most popular of the big knives among buckskinners all over the country is the bowie (Figure 6-1). The classic broad-bladed, clip-pointed design is actually centuries older than the Louisiana rogue and Texas patriot it was belatedly named for.

Jim Bowie earned his reputation as a mean man with a blade during a fracas on a Mississippi River sandbar in 1827. You've undoubtedly heard the tale of how his brother Rezin had given him the prototype for the bowie knife just before Jim was called upon to lop off assorted appendages

A buckskinning family enjoys an afternoon at the 'hawk block. Tomahawk and knife throwing aren't just for men; women and kids enjoy these activities, also.

of his enemies. Actually, that knife—in Rezin's own words—was a short Spanish-style cutlass, now called a "searles," common in the former Spanish territory of Louisiana.

But Col. Bowie had evidently adopted the classic bowie shape before he died wielding it at the Alamo in 1836. By then, that style of knife was already being called a bowie, and they were as common as belts in the South.

There's some question as to whether bowie knives were that familiar on the northern plains and in the Rocky Mountains during that period. In his excellent book, *Firearms, Traps, & Tools of the Mountain Men*, historian Carl P. Russell says they probably weren't. He cites the offer, made by an English cutlery in late 1836, to use the "Texian knives" for trade items. According to Russell, an official of the American Fur Company declined because, "The article is not wanted yet in our region."

On the other hand, artist Alfred Jacob Miller, who was at the 1837 rendezvous, made the following note of items a fur trapper would outfit himself with before setting out for the fall trapping: "In addition to his animals he procures 5 or 6 traps (usually carried in a trap-sack), ammunition, a few pounds of tobacco, a supply of moccasins, a wallet called a 'possible sack,' gun, *bowie knife*, [my italics] and sometimes a tomahawk."

Now, Miller had come to the mountains from New Orleans, so maybe he called all big knives bowies. Or maybe the American Fur Company official quoted by Russell wasn't the best of all judges as to what the mountaineers preferred in blades. In any case, if the dog soldiers started shaking folks down at modern rendezvous and confiscating bowies for lack of authenticity, it's my guess it would take several fifty-five gallon drums to hold them all.

More authentic, if less common today, would certainly be an "Arkansas toothpick" or some other form of large dagger. According to Russell, naval dirks were also popular with the beaver men, as were the broad "dags" sold without handles to the Indians for use as knives or spear points. And the saber-like "rifleman's knife" of the eastern longhunter was still in use (Figure 6-1).

Green River Knives

The pure fighting knives were not really that functional for anything else. The all-around knife of the mountain fur trade was a cheap butcher knife manufactured specifically for the Indian trade. These large, thin-bladed,

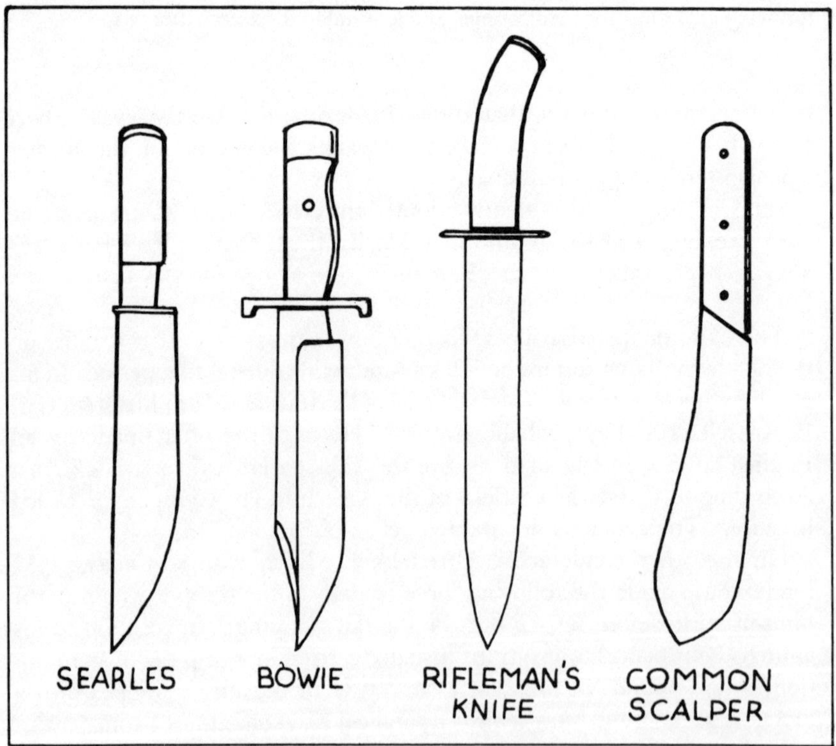

FIGURE 6–1 Basic knife shapes.

hiltless knives were called "scalpers" (Figure 6-1) after one of their more gristly uses. But they were also called upon to flesh hides, cut rope, whittle wood, and do countless other camp and trail chores. They were frequently carried in wide scabbards studded with brass tacks and engulfing half or more of the handles.

If a 'skinner is savvy enough to carry such a trade knife, he'll probably insist on the name Green River.

The Green River in present-day Wyoming was the scene of a half-dozen rendezvous during the fur trade. The name came to represent the way the world ought to be: plenty of grass for the animals and plunder for the trappers. "Up to Green River" meant a thing met the most exacting of standards. By a pair of coincidences, though, there developed a slight variation on that meaning of the phrase.

The most successful American manufacturer of trade knives, John Russell, located his factory on the banks of the Green River in Massachusetts, and his products bore the legend "Green River Works" on the blades. Earlier English-made knives had been stamped with the initials "G.R.," which stood for *Georgius Rex* in honor of the monarch. Not thinking of King George, many of the trappers simply considered the letters to stand for Green River.

And so by the flickering fire, when many a red miscreant met his fate again and again, the saying was coined that the hero had "sunk my knife in him, right up to Green River!" It worked equally well whether it was a Russell knife or an English one. And again, to these hardened lads, it meant a satisfactory end to things—the way the world ought to be.

The J. Russell and Company line of knives is still being produced, now in Roosevelt, Utah. Like the point blankets of the Hudson's Bay Company, they have proven fit for ages.

Throwing Knives

The one type of knife in the 'skinner's arsenal that I suspect is a thoroughly modern invention is the rough throwing blade. I say "rough" because it would be foolhardy to subject a fine knife to the abuses of chunkin'. A blade with enough spring in it to withstand being slammed against solid wood time and again isn't likely to hold much of an edge. A hilt is the first thing that would break off, so throwing knives don't have them. The handle would be next. Many throwing knives have thick leather panels held in place with rivets. I can't prove it, you understand, but it just doesn't seem likely that a mountain man would have messed around with such an overall worthless piece of hardware.

No matter, throwing knives are a lot of fun. And you just about have to have a specialized chunker if you want to compete with the big kids at the rendezvous.

The typical 'skinner's throwing knife is big, and designed to be thrown by the handle instead of the blade as they do in the movies. Experts in knife throwing recommend you select one that's as long and heavy as your tomahawk. That way you can use the same amount of force and throw from about the same distance as you do with your 'hawk. The practice that you do with one, in effect, will serve for the other.

The throwing knife needs to be balanced, too, so that when it's placed on your outstretched finger like a seesaw on its fulcrum, the knife should be horizontal when your finger's in the middle. The best way to adjust the balance of your throwing knife is by changing the handle—using lighter material or less of it if the knife is handle-heavy, and vice versa.

Most people find it harder to learn to throw a knife than a tomahawk for some reason. That's if they don't know how to use either one. However, once they learn to stick the 'hawk, knife throwing seems to fall right into place. We'll get into chunkin' a little later. But before we leave the subject of buckskinning knives, there are two others that deserve mention.

Many 'skinners carry small, razor-sharp knives sheathed on their hunting pouches, or otherwise handy, for the sole purpose of trimming patches for their rifles. There are two good reasons for having a separate patch knife: It doesn't get put to rougher uses and therefore maintains that sharp edge longer; and since you aren't going to leave it by the fire after you've peeled onions, it's always where you can lay your hand on it when you need it.

Straight razors frequently get adapted to this purpose. The folding handle is discarded, and a portion of the blade is ground down and encased in a rigid handle of antler, bone, or wood.

Speaking of folding knives, don't overlook the convenience of clasp or pocket knives. They've been around a long time, since way before the first Ashley-Henry crew left St. Louis. My absolute favorite knife, for everything from peeling potatoes to peeling a deer, is a wooden-handled folder with a three-inch, drop-point Solengen blade.

Most pilgrims will already have knives, like my folder, which they can use modified or as-is with their primitive gear. For the guy just getting into it, the whole topic of knives is probably boring anyway. What most pilgrims are fascinated with, can't wait to put their hands on, is a genuine Indian tomahawk!

The European "Tomahack"

Although it was indeed cherished by the Indians, the common tomahawk is of ancient European design. (Exceptions should probably be granted to the wicked-looking Missouri war hatchet and to the pipe tomahawk, obviously designed with the Indians in mind.) A light, rakish hatchet

A veteran 'skinner shows a pilgrim the ropes. A newcomer need never go without advice, cheerfully given, at buckskinning events.

evolved on the Spanish coast of the Bay of Biscay, where ore deposits spawned a metal-working industry nearly two thousand years ago. By the time Europeans started trading with the Indians of the New World, the common ax in use throughout Europe had the classic tomahawk shape. The traders merely picked some light ones that they thought would be useful to the Indians and packed them in the holds of westbound ships.

Naturally, the Indians were delighted with the metal hatchets. They had developed a similar tool/weapon on their own, but with stone instead of metal heads. Some Algonquian people in Virginia called this stone ax, and the later metal ones, by a name that sounded like "tomahack" to the European settlers. Thus the ancient European ax comes down to us as a tomahawk, indelibly linked to the Indians.

The colonists used them too, of course. Military units on both sides of the Atlantic were issued "tomahawks" and the settlers had a lot of woodcutting to do.

That monumental task—clearing the great North American forests—led to the development of the Yankee ax, which more than made up in efficiency as a tree-feller and hammer what it had lost as a last-ditch weapon. By the early 1800s, this uniquely American tool had taken the shape it has today: short, wide blade with most of the mass centered around the handle. By the time of the Western Fur Trade Era, most American backwoodsmen, including the mountain men, were probably carrying a hatchet that looked like one you could buy at a hardware or sporting-goods store today, except that the handle was straight instead of curved.

There were plenty of tomahawks in the Rockies, to be sure. They were still a hot item in the Indian trade, and the French-Canadians apparently preferred them. But the trapper with his roots east of the Missouri likely favored the more efficient design of the Yankee ax.

Today, the tomahawk is solidly entrenched in buckskinning. They're much more fun to chunk than a modern ax, and they just *look* right. The buckskinning supply houses and a good many gun stores that sell muzzleloaders stock tomahawks. Generally, you'll find the lighter-weight cast-steel models are better chunkers while the stronger forged type makes a better camp tool. Some of the forged models, however, have a "weeping heart" or some other design stamped out of the blade, which lightens the weight and improves the balance without significantly altering its use as a tool.

When it comes to camping, I use a Yankee ax set on a straight tomahawk handle. It does a better job of cutting firewood and pounding down tent stakes, and it's authentic. For play, though, I turn to my cast-steel New Reliable 'hawk.

Whichever type of tomahawk you buy, if you plan to do much throwing, go ahead and buy yourself some extra handles at the outset. You *are* going to be busting them.

A large slab from a tree trunk makes an excellent throwing block for tomahawks and knives. You should keep the background free of spectators since a bad throw can bounce wildly; and never stick blades in a live tree.

Throwing 'Hawks and Knives

Tomahawk throwing is fairly easy to learn—at least to the extent that you can consistently stick it from your well-worn "spot." The best way to get started is to have someone who is good at it show you what he or she does. At the rendezvous, the person to ask for help is the one who hangs around the throwing block whether there's anything going on or not. A 'skinner is always happy to give advice to a pilgrim. Don't be shy about asking.

Even a *good* teacher can lead you just so far into chunkin', though. The rest you have to do on your own. And I don't believe there's any formula, either. I've read and been told that if your tomahawk handle is X inches long, it should make one revolution in Y feet, two revolutions in Z feet.

If you're sticking the 'hawk too high on the blade with the handle jutting back toward you *(top)*, you should move a little closer to the target. If the handle is nearly touching the block *(bottom, left)*, move away from the target. When you throw from the correct distance, your tomahawk handle should be nearly parallel with the block when it sticks *(bottom, right)*.

The only thing I can tell you in good conscience is to stand up there and throw the darn thing. And if it sticks, pay attention to where you were standing when you turned it loose and keep throwing from that spot.

If the 'hawk is hitting handle-first, back up; if it's bouncing off the head, move in. Sooner or later, you'll find your distance.

Of course that's assuming you're doing everything the same for each throw. The key is to be consistent with the force of your throw, the length of arc you scribe with your swing, the point at which you release, the *way* you release, and so on. If you succeed in keeping everything the same (a tall order), you should be able to stick a 'hawk from the same spot all day long.

Grip the handle like a golf club, with your thumb extended rather than wrapped around. That allows you to release it cleanly, like soap slipping from your hand.

After he releases the 'hawk, the fingers of the author's right hand are still curled as if around the handle. That's because the 'hawk has slipped free smoothly, almost like a bar of soap.

Everyone works out his own little hop-and-skip routine, sort of like a bowler's approach, which delivers him to the throwing spot with some momentum behind him. As a right-hander, I start out with my right foot slightly forward, step out with it as I'm drawing back, then swing as I'm stepping forward on the left foot. I find myself in a semicrouch after every good, solid throw.

I also find that locking my elbow at about half-cock, swinging back as far behind my right ear as I can, and making my forward swing directly over my right shoulder helps me keep my throws consistent. All the while my left arm is immobilized as though in a sling. But I see others as good or better with a tomahawk who swing their 'hawks nearly sideways and let their free arms flap. It's just a matter of what works for you.

Flipping the wrist downward to impart extra spin, or upward to dampen spin is strictly for the experts. Beginners should release the handle "dead," with a locked wrist.

Typically, you'll find you have two "spots," one for a single revolution and another farther back for two. When you can free yourself from the bounds of set distances and consistent movements, that's when you're *really* good! And you would have to be really good for a tomahawk to be useful to you as a thrown weapon. Suppose an irate Blackfoot suddenly pops out of the brush with bow drawn. You don't have time to hop and

The stiff-arm, stiff-leg method of tomahawk throwing. Everyone develops his own style of wind-up and delivery. (Photo by John Wootters)

skip, let alone find your "spot." That's when you flip your wrist one way or the other to adjust the spin of the 'hawk to the distance rather than the other way around.

For most of us, it's challenging enough just to find our "spot" with nothing more than a little embarrassment in the balance.

Throwing a knife involves essentially the same process as does throwing a 'hawk. If your knife matches your tomahawk in length and weight, theoretically you should be able to use the same "spot." Again, it's easier if you start with the 'hawk.

In throwing either one of them, remember that you're playing a dangerous game. A bad throw could bounce a surprising distance, so make sure the area around the block is clear. And *please* don't throw at live trees.

Making Primitive Sheaths

You shouldn't walk around with an unsheathed 'hawk in your belt any more than you would stick an unsheathed knife in your pocket. A simple "envelope" sheath is easy to make out of rawhide or thick leather. Simply fold the material into a rough triangle around the blade of the 'hawk and tie it. (See Figure 6-2).

Being in the Texas Army, I feel somewhat obligated to pack around a bowie from time to time. The Connecticut Valley Arms kit suits me fine, but I don't much care for the sheath that comes with it. So I covered it in thin rawhide from the flank of a doe. I soaked the rawhide, stretched it, and sewed it on with artificial sinew. It dried taut and smooth. I painted it Indian-style with Chinese vermillion and chrome yellow trade paints (acrylics, actually, but the colors are historically correct) and gave it a light coat of beef tallow and beeswax to ward off moisture. You could give just about any modern knife sheath that treatment and it would pass muster at the rendezvous.

Many of today's mountain men follow the example set by the old-time trappers and carry as a belt knife a scalper or common butcher knife, either from J. Russell & Co. or the local discount store. And the favored way of carrying it, as it was then, is in a wide sheath of heavy leather adorned with brass tacks.

Two characteristics of this plains Indian scabbard are that only a portion of the handle sticks out above it and that it has a single slit or opening through which the belt passes. The knife and that portion of the sheath that contains it are snugged between the belt and the wearer's body (Figure 6-3).

To make a pattern, lay your knife so that the handle sticks over one edge of a piece of paper about halfway. That edge corresponds to the top of your sheath. Draw a straight line next to the back of the blade and perpendicu-

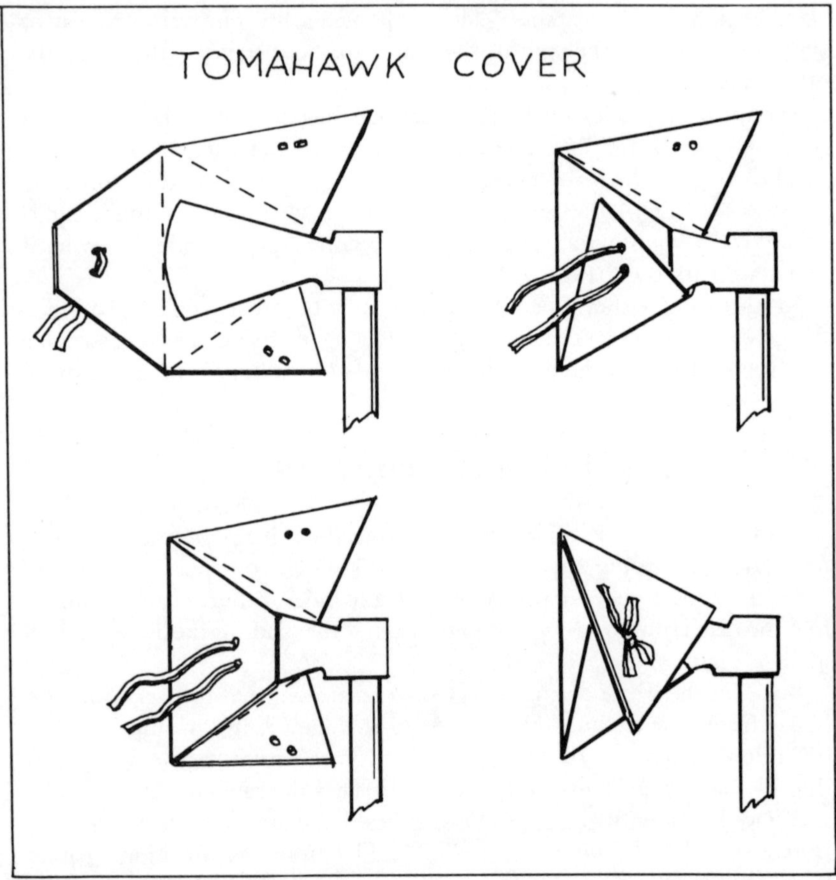

FIGURE 6–2   Making a tomahawk cover.

lar to the edge of the paper. That's where the sheath will fold. Fold the paper and sketch out the shape you want your sheath to take. Allow plenty of room since these sheaths are normally more than twice the width of the blades they carry.

Cut out the pattern and transfer it to heavy leather (at least eight-ounce stuff if you want to use tacks in it). Mark where you want the slit for your belt—usually about where the knife's blade and handle join. Cut and trim the leather piece, and cut out the belt slit. If the leather needs finishing, this is the time to do it.

Fold the sheath over the blade and glue the edges together with something waterproof. Now you're ready to put in the tacks. (See Figure 6-3).

Make sure you're getting tacks with brass heads, not just brass-coated. That coating will wear off and then what you'll have is rust spots. Brass trade tacks are sold by all the buckskinner stores. They come in several sizes and with both rounded and cone-shaped surfaces.

What they all have in common is that the shaft breaks loose from the head when you try to bend it over and secure it in the back of the sheath. A

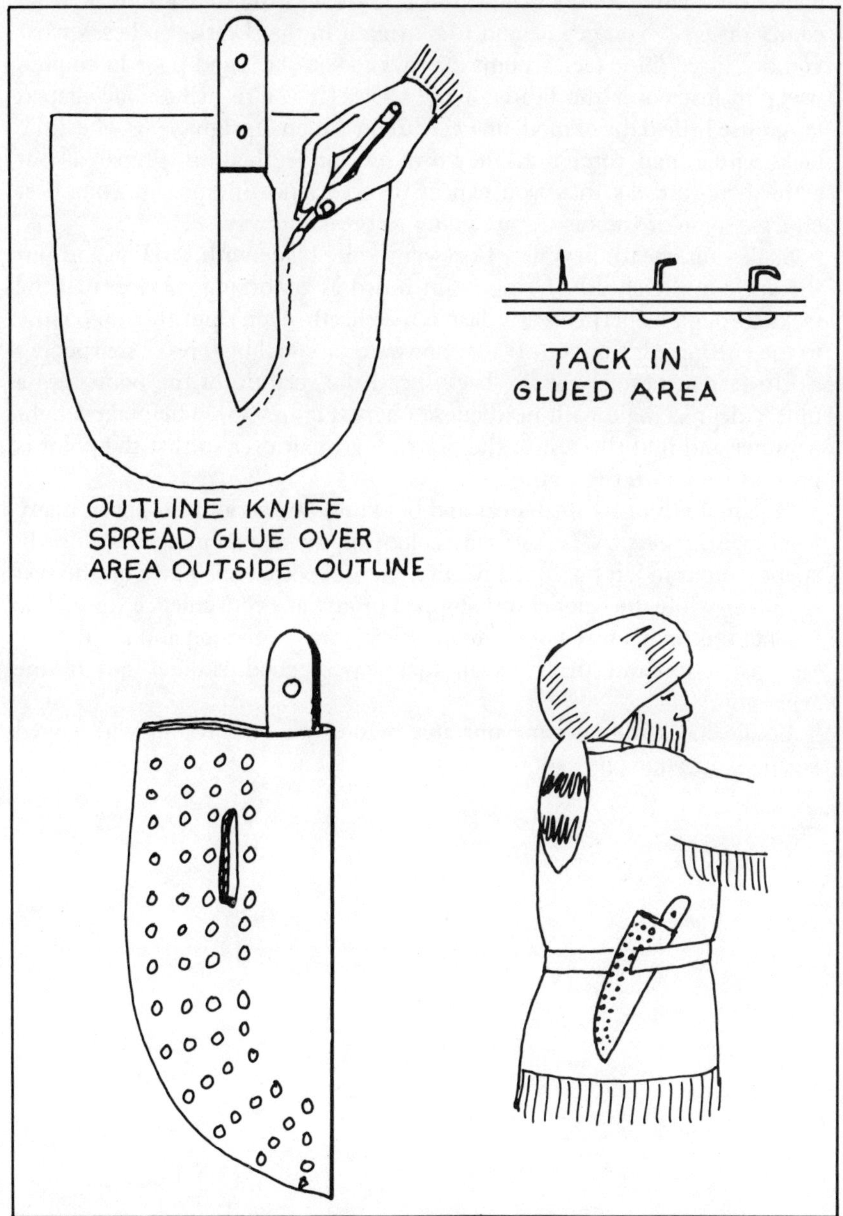

FIGURE 6–3 Making a knife sheath.

great aggravation. Over the years they have found ways to make tack shafts harder, but I guess there's only so much you can do with solder.

An obvious solution is to anneal the tack shaft by heating it with a small propane torch until it turns red, then allowing it to cool slowly. That makes the shaft soften, all right, but it also melts the solder and the head comes off *before* you get around to putting it in the sheath. So here's what you do: Place some tacks, point up, in a cookie sheet and pour in enough water to just cover the heads of the tacks. (If you're using cone-shaped tacks, use little dabs of modeling clay to hold them upright.) Now heat the tacks with a small torch until they turn red and let them sit. Prepare about a third more tacks than you expect to need since in spite of your best efforts, some of the rascals are going to break anyway.

Soak your sheath in water. Coat your knife blade with vaseline and put the knife in the sheath. Using a soft board as a working surface, nail the tacks through to permanently fasten the sheath. Don't put them too close to the cutting edge of your blade, however, or you'll be forever sharpening it. To fasten the tacks at the back, bend the very tip of the point into a ninety-degree angle with needlenose pliers (Figure 6-3). Then take a light hammer and fold the rest of the protruding shaft over so that the point is pressed back into the leather.

One more thing: Tomahawks and big knives are serious no-nos in many legal jurisdictions. A Texas Army colonel of my acquaintance very nearly spent a night in jail because a deputy sheriff spotted his 'hawk on the seat of his car while the colonel was stopped briefly at a convenience store. The colonel was on his way home for an official Army function and the deputy was patriotic—and that was all that kept a good 'skinner out of the hoosegow.

Better check the laws in your area before you venture out with edged weapons in your possession.

7

Dressing to Fit In

There are a lot of folks who are interested, maybe even involved in muzzleloading who are prime candidates for buckskinning. Yet they don't join in. Some don't have the time. Others feel they can't justify buying another, more authentic, gun. But you know what holds a surprising number back? They don't have a *thing* to wear.

A major part of buckskinning is wearing the clothing of the period you're recreating, and you can't buy it off the rack in very many places. You can outfit yourself head-to-toe through the buckskinning specialty shops listed in this chapter, but at greater expense than most newcomers will want to incur.

Blending in at a primitive event isn't really that difficult. Most 'skinners are friendly folks who welcome new faces into their circle. But they are serious about recreating an aura of the 1800s mountain rendezvous, and the presence of pork-eaters in blue jeans and nylon windbreakers—or worse, in unauthentic halloween costumes—cheapens their efforts. With a little thought and the clothes you have in your closet, you can be ready for rendezvous right now.

The Well-Dressed Pilgrim

The first rule for the beginner is to be understated. Conservative. I'll grant that many buckskinners are positively gaudy in their appearance, but these guys are emulating the free trappers, who, when they went to rendezvous, did tend to put on the dog a little. A veteran 'skinner knows *how* to be gaudy.

Instead of trying to look like Ol' Bill Williams right away, the beginner is better off concentrating simply on looking like he belongs in the time period. After all, there were newcomers at all those historic rendezvous, too.

With his jeans and Reservation Period beadwork, this young man has a way to go before he's correctly attired for the Western Fur Trade Era, but at least he's making the effort.

Any shirt of simple design, especially a pullover, will do for starters if it's of a solid, basic color. Take off the breast pockets and if the collar doesn't look right, turn it under. Square-tailed shirts are nice because you can wear them with the tails out to cover the more modern aspects of your trousers, such as the zipper fly and machine-stitched belt loops. Gray, black, tan, brown, or navy trousers are all fine.

Blue jeans are anathema at a rendezvous. Jeans didn't appear until later in history, and then they were first worn almost exclusively by miners in the California gold fields. Jeans of other colors might pass, but I would advise you to get out a razor blade and take off those hip pockets.

I used to have an old pair of Levis in a sand color that were so worn they had a nap to them like buckskin. One sweltering Saturday, the Texas Army mustered to fire a few salutes during the opening of a museum at an old homestead, which had been restored by the local historical society. The only period trousers I had then were heavy wool, and it was way too hot for that. So I wore my sand-colored Levis. Otherwise I was pretty authentic in beaded buckskin shirt, moccasins, and beaver topper. I let my shirt hang out to hide my jeans.

The Texas Army is a pretty backwoodsy crew when we turn out in full uniform. With our rifles and bowies, we attracted more attention than the old house. Even the fiercely knowledgeable old ladies of the historical society were impressed, and they gave us a special tour.

But when I filed by one of the women in the house, she looked down and saw those distinctive Levis pockets peeking out from under my shirt and she snatched me out of line like an auto worker plucking a deformed hood ornament off the conveyor belt. *That* was when I learned all about the miners in California.

For footgear, a pair of plain slip-on boots is perfect. *Not* cowboy boots, though, unless you want a lecture on the history of ranching. Almost any type of leather shoes except wing tips can be rendered acceptable with the addition of a pair of *botas*, bell-shaped Spanish leggings that tie just below the knee and hang down, covering all of your foot except your toes. A little experimentation with a pair of scissors and the newspaper will produce a pattern, and you can use wool, white canvas, or leather for the leggings. Trim of red or navy serge or wool would be appropriate, and you can dress them up further with conchos, tin cones, and the like.

Real hivernants wear moccasins. They're the first item of clothing the beginning buckskinner ought to buy or make.

To top off your outfit, an old felt hat—a cowboy hat or old fedora— looks right if you steam the crown flat on top, or to its original round shape. Make the brim flat like a Smokey Bear hat, or turn it up in front, or get out the garden hose and make it slouch all around. Remove any obviously modern hat band, but you don't *need* to replace it with a beaded one. Nor is it absolutely necessary to stick a feather in it.

This Texas Army medic is wearing store-bought clothes that could reasonably pass for 1836 styles. Many men at the original mountain rendezvous wore store clothes. It usually wasn't until the store clothes wore out that the mountain men switched to buckskins.

This 'skinner is wearing buckskin-colored jeans, disguised by his shirttails and *botas*, Spanish-style leggings. Trousers are usually the last article of primitive clothing acquired, and some veteran 'skinners avoid skins and wool in warm weather.

Cold and rainy weather really separates the hivernants from the pork-eaters. To be truthful, many otherwise well-equipped 'skinners are forced into down jackets and modern slickers when the skies turn nasty.

You can go a long way toward licking the cold and wet with a simple poncho fashioned out of an old wool blanket. Make a T-shaped cut in the center and sew ties on either side of the vertical line of the T for closing it up at the neck (Figure 7-1). Wearing your belt or sash on the outside will keep the poncho from flapping in the breeze, or sew ties on the sides, front and back. Army surplus stores are a good place to find cheap used blankets of from eighty to eighty-five percent reconstituted wool. I have found them in maroon, gray, brown, navy, and white, all colors that fit in at rendezvous. Don't show up in olive drab—you would look more at home on the set of M*A*S*H.

When you add your hunting pouch and horn, and maybe a scalper and

A top hat, moccasins, and calico shirt—and you're primitive. The author is dressed up to stalk the wily cat squirrel.

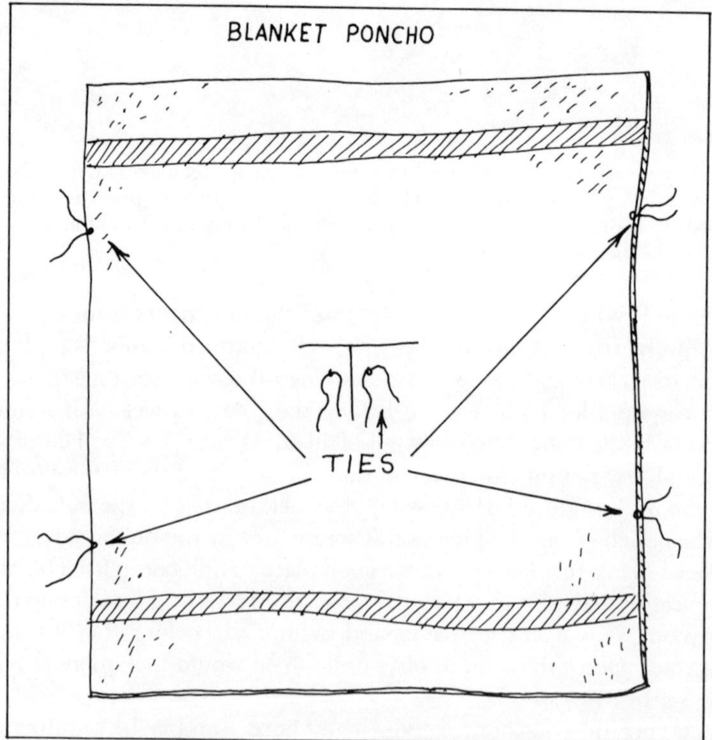

FIGURE 7–1   Design of a simple blanket poncho.

'hawk to the above clothing, you'll blend in pretty well. You won't look like a graduate mountain man, but you will be demonstrating your willingness to participate in creating the illusion of time travel.

Most 'skinners will bend over backward to welcome a newcomer who is willing to learn. Rendezvous large and small usually provide a modern camping area for those who are there to get their feet wet a toe at a time. Nobody expects the modern campers to dress like Jim Bridger. Just meet us halfway.

Here's a sample rendezvous dress code, this one from the Texas Association of Buckskinners, which is relatively liberal in such matters:

A simple bandana makes suitable primitive headgear. Even old 'skinners like Paul "Tanglefoot" Berry of the *Trade Blanket* staff favor it when the weather is warm.

When modern campers visit the primitive camp the same period of dress should be worn as is mandatory in the primitive camp. However, we realize many do not yet have such dress. Please do not come into the primitive camp wearing the following apparel:

1. Shorts
2. T-shirts
3. Sandals or tennis shoes
4. Modern cowboy hats (kikker)
5. Short-sleeved shirts
6. Blue Levis (they are unsightly in photos)
7. Nylon-coated windbreakers & down vests

It is easy for men to fit in with long-sleeved shirts, brown pants (almost any basic color—even plaids) and boots. Women with long dresses are fine and if it's cool, a shawl of some sort.

If you refuse these standards—don't come. If you can't meet these standards—come, and have a good time with us!

Trappers, Traders, and Missionaries

When you're ready to plunge into mountain toggery, you can tailor your clothing after what we know of the mountain men's garb, or you can wear what all the other well-dressed 'skinners are wearing these days. If you study both approaches, you will find some differences. But they're minor, the effects of fashion trends you'll find in any social circle.

Nowadays many 'skinners lean heavily toward Indian clothing, complete with breechclouts. Historian Jack Sunder of Austin, Texas, author of *Bill Sublette, Mountain Man* and other books on the western fur trade, told me he doesn't think the mountain men were nearly as smitten with the Indian culture as we buckskinners are. Even those with Indian wives, who were excellent seamstresses by most accounts, would have them tailor their clothing in the white man's fashion, Sunder said.

Here's one eyewitness account of what the fur trappers wore, from Osborne Russell:

His personal dress is a flannel or cotton shirt (if he is fortunate enough to obtain one, if not antelope skin answers the purpose of over and undershirt), a pair of leather breeches with blanket or smoked buffalo skin leggins, a coat made of blanket or buffalo robe, a hat or cap of wool, buffalo or otter skin, his hose are pieces of blanket wrapped around his feet, which are covered with a pair of moccasins made of dressed deer, elk or buffalo skin, with his long hair falling loosely over his shoulders, completes his uniform.

Michael "Two Bears" Hughes displays the latest rage in buckskinning style: the Indian breechclout. Its proponents claim coolness and comfort heretofore unknown by white men. They have a point, since few trappers were likely to have gone quite so far in emulating the Indians.

Here's another view, from Philip Edwards, a member of a Methodist mission which stopped in at the 1834 rendezvous:

> To form an adequate conception of their apparel, you must see it. A suit of clothes is seldom washed or turned from the time it is first worn until it is laid aside. Caps and hats are made of beaver and otter skins, the skins of buffalo calves &c. Some of these are fantastically ornamented with tails and horns. These ornaments may be badges of distinction, for aught that I know, but being a stranger in the country, I am not able to speak decidedly. You will perhaps recollect to have seen in the "far west" of our own United States, the buckskin hunting shirt and leggins gracefully hung with fringes along the arms and sides. But I am sure you have never seen the tasty fashion of fringes carried to perfection. Here they are six or seven inches long, and hung densely on every seam, I believe, both of the hunting shirt and leggins.

(Here both Edwards and Russell mention "leggins," the crotchless trousers the Indians wore with their breechclouts. But you'll notice the

According to one eye-witness account, rows of heavy fringe, hanging "densely on every seam," were the height of fashion among Rocky Mountain trappers, as shown in this Alfred Jacob Miller painting. (Courtesy of The Walters Art Gallery, Baltimore, Maryland)

Bill Tyler (Charlton Heston) leaves the rendezvous wearing a store-bought shirt and Hudson's Bay blanket capote. Henry Frapp (Brian Keith), who spent his season's earnings on women and watered-down liquor, is riding out the same way he rode in. (Courtesy of Columbia Pictures)

trapper in the Russell account was also wearing breeches. Apparently he would wear the leggins as what we call chaps. Indeed, in nineteenth-century Texas, at least, chaps were called leggins.)

I reckon you get the point. A Rocky Mountain trapper wore what he could get. He bought a red flannel shirt at rendezvous and wore it until it fell off of him. Then he traded some sweet Flathead lass out of an elk one. Or if he was the marryin' kind, he talked his wife into sewing one up for him. Or if he didn't truck with the Indians, maybe he did it himself.

Not all the mountain men were trappers who spent year after year in the high country. Traders like Sublette and Campbell returned to St. Louis in the fall to sell pelts and obtain supplies for the following summer's rendezvous. They may have worn moccasins for comfort in the stirrups, and they may have worn buckskins for fashion, but you can bet they were well-tailored ones.

In later years there were adventurers and missionaries at the rendezvous. The adventurers probably dressed Early L.L. Bean. And if you believe Hollywood, missionaries have always dressed like Johnny Cash.

Ladies of the Mountains

Until 1836, when Narcissa Whitman and Eliza Spalding accompanied their missionary husbands west, there were only Indian women at the rendezvous. Snakes, Flatheads, Nez Perces. Maybe a Crow and Ute or two. The basic garb for the mountain Indian lass is a tunic, knee-high leggings, and moccasins. The dresses could be made from some sort of trade cloth—wool, cotton flannel, calico—or of skins. The leggings would most likely be wool or skins. If you made a dress that was constructed something like a poncho, laced or sewn up the sides, with wide half-sleeves, you wouldn't be far off. For details, consult *Primitive Indian Dresses* by Susan Fecteau.

I confess a blissful ignorance of the subtle variety available to the woman who would emulate Narcissa. The only thing I can tell you about the dresses of these "white women" I see at the rendezvous is that they're all long. Another book on the matter is *Feminine Fur Trade Fashions* by Kathryn J. Wilson and James A. Hanson.

Indian dresses of buckskin and trade cloth. These tunics, simple in design but sometimes highly embellished, are usually worn with leggings or high-top moccasins. Cowries, tin cones, and applique of ribbon are common decorations.

A reasonable stab at what white women on the Oregon Trail might have worn. The specs, however, are modern. Until 1836, there were no white women at the rendezvous. The appearance of missionaries that year heralded new fashion trends in the mountains.

Whiskers and Specs

For a while in the recent history of buckskinning, there was a mild controversy, or at least confusion, over whether mountain men wore whiskers.

Many of the paintings of mountain men, and of course the photographs, were made well after the Western Fur Trade Era, at a time when most men wore beards. Most 'skinners at one point assumed that all mountain men wore facial hair.

Later, others realized that during the period in history, beards were out of style in the United States. Thumb through your kid's history book and look at the pictures if you doubt that; Jackson, Crockett, Webster, Houston, none of these guys had beards. Moreover, there is evidence that the Indians detested whiskers, calling those who wore them "dogfaces."

A hard line developed among some 'skinners to the effect that *no* self-respecting mountain man would wear a beard, and the battle line was drawn. Mostly, it fell between those 'skinners with whiskers and those without.

But wait a minute. If nobody wore a beard, who did the Indians have to call a "dogface?" Cooler heads leafed through the works of Alfred Jacob Miller, an eyewitness, and guess what they found? Right. Some mountain men wore beards. And some didn't. In fact, those shaggy mountaineers so defamed by the Indians have been given some credit for starting the trend that, by the Civil War, had put whiskers on almost every male face able to sprout them.

The obvious fact that many buckskinners wear glasses hasn't prompted any controversy that I know of over whether any mountain men were nearsighted. There were spectacles in those days, of course, little bitty ones in wire frames. According to Dr. L.D. Bronson, in *Early American Specs*, sunglasses were around then, too. Available in green, blue, and gray.

The last thing anyone would holler for the dog soldiers about is your glasses. Too many people need them and too few will go to the expense—and bother, I might add—of wearing those little watch-crystal jobs. You'll

This eastern longhunter is wearing modern glasses that nonetheless fit in well with his homespun rifleman's coat and Scots-Irish tam. Frames of a more modern design would ruin his outfit. (Photo by Gene Hyre)

see fellows—dressed in carefully researched war shirts made of deerskins they brain-tanned themselves after killing the deer with patched round balls they cast themselves—wearing modern specs right out of a Foster Grant ad.

It's a problem. Modern glasses ruin a good outfit, no doubt about it. I'm nearsighted myself, but I wear simple wire frames, sort of like John Denver's, so I haven't felt pressed to remedy the situation. I'll probably go ahead and buy some old-timey frames. You can still pick up originals at flea markets for considerably less than you have to pay for the latest fashions in eyewear.

Contact lenses offer an obvious solution. I used to wear them, but I quit. Rolling out of Hudson's Bay blankets of a morning, sitting there for a minute in red longjohns, gazing nearsightedly at the quiet lodges in the pale golden mist, then digging out some plastic bottles of cleansing and wetting solutions—it just doesn't fit in.

The Merchants of Buckskinning

If you think the trade blankets at the rendezvous hold some goodies, wait until you look through the catalogs from some of the buckskinning supply houses. You will be amazed and delighted. The best way I know to get an idea of who is selling what is to check the ads in publications like *Black Powder Times*, *The Buckskin Report*, *Muzzle Blasts*, *Muzzleloader*, and *Trade Blanket*.

Here's a list, regretfully but unavoidably incomplete, of folks who can outfit you for the mountains:

Avalon Forge
409 Gun Rd.
Baltimore, MD 21227

Bitterroot Trading Post
910 N. 1st St.
Hamilton, MT 59840

Blue-Eyes-Shoots Co.
1809 Ravenwood Dr.
Concord, CA 94520

Buckskin Supply Co.
Box B
Cherokee, TX 76832

The Buffalo Bull
Box 8
Marion, IA 52302

Buffalo Hoof Trading Co.
Box 103
Gowrie, IA 50543

Buffalo Robe Indian Trading Post
18555 Sherman Way
Reseda, CA 91335

Cash Mfg. Co.
816 S. Division St.
Waunakee, WI 53597

Crazy Crow
107 N. Fannin
Denison, TX 75020

Dixie Gun Works
Gunpowder Lane
Union City, TN 38261

Eagle Feather Trading Post
(Dept. TBN)
706 W. Riverdale Rd.
Ogden, UT 84037

The Flintlock
1238 South Beach Blvd.
Anaheim, CA 92804

You can find some ready-made primitive clothing, such as calico shirts, around many trade blankets at rendezvous. But if you can't find what you want there, dozens of buckskinning supply houses are available to complete your primitive wardrobe.

Fort Green Ville Trading Company
2 Front Drive
Little Hocking, OH 45742

French Lick Trading Co.
Box 825
Gallatin, TN 37066

Golden Age Arms
Box 283
Delaware, OH 43015

The Great Northwest Fur & Trading Post
Box 88
Heron, MT 59844

Grey Owl
113-15 Springfield Blvd.
Queens Village, NY 11429

Indian Ridge Traders
Box 869
Royal Oak, MI 48068

Log Cabin Shop
Box 275
Lodi, OH 44254

Lou's Leathers
Rt. 1, Box 176-A
Elk Horn, KY 42733

Medicine Mountain Trading Company
Box 124
Sturgis, SD 57785

Moccasin Heaven
112 East Kossuth
Columbus, OH 43206

Mountain State Muzzleloading Supply
Box 154-1B
Williamstown, WV 26187

Northwest Outpost
520 South Hayes
Moscow, ID 83840

Northwest Traders
4999 Packard Dr.
Dayton, OH 45424

October Country
Box 142
Gardner, CO 81040

La Pelleterie de Fort de Chartres
Fort de Chartres State Historic Site-M
Prairie du Rocher, IL 62277

Salish House, Inc.
Box 27
Rollins, MT 59931

Tecumseh's Trading Post
Box 369
Shartlesville, PA 19554

Track of the Wolf Co.
7445 Zane Ave. N.
Brooklyn Park, MN 55429

Trappers Rendezvous
Box 8822
Denver, CO 80201

Treaty Oak Indian Store, Inc.
Box 5743
Jacksonville, FL 32207

Upper Missouri Trading Co.
Crofton, NE 68730

Wahkon Bay Co.
Rt. 1, Box 101B
Wahkon, MN 56386

8

Dressing "Flauntingly"

Some of the haughty free trappers, Joe Meek tells us, dressed "flauntingly." And why shouldn't you? After all, you're holding your own in the shooting matches. You're getting to be a pretty fair hand around a primitive camp, deft with flint and steel. You've made meat. You're beginning to *feel* like a mountain man.

What's more, you have done enough reading in the literature of the Western Fur Trade Era, and the biographies and the histories, that you have a sense of who and what you would have been if you had lived back then. It's time you started expressing yourself a little in your rendezvous togs.

You can buy every stitch from traders if you like, and have absolutely no cause to be ashamed of it. That's what the mountain men did. On the other hand, you may want to cut costs and make many of the items yourself. That way you get exactly what you want, not just a selection from a catalog. And there's tremendous pride to be derived from a nicely finished article of dress that is the product of your own imagination, research, and toil. A shirt, say, from skins you tanned from animals you stalked and took is as much a big-game trophy as any mounted head on the wall. Furs, feathers, bones, and antlers that are involved in your personal history in that way can all be utilized. Like the Indians, a 'skinner wastes nothing.

Basic Materials and Tools

You're not limited to skins and furs, though, nor are they always the most desirable materials for primitive garb. When the mountain man could get textiles, he used them. In the interest of authenticity, you should stick with the same materials, or close approximations, that went to the rendezvous in the trade caravans. The following is a list of the main raw materials that form the buckskinner's haberdashery:

108

Wool. You can still buy the 100-percent virgin wool blankets the old-time trappers bought, but they are expensive. Blankets of eighty to eighty-five percent reprocessed wool make more sense. Navy, gray, and chestnut are common colors, and they're perfectly fine for the rendezvous period. Just stay away from olive drab. If you do much primitive camping in cold and wet weather, you'll find blanketing far superior to buckskins.

Skins or leather. Store-bought leather is awfully expensive, which is why so many 'skinners are just that, and tanners to boot. Processing your own hides is a lot of work, and only you can determine if it's worth it. On the plus side, skin clothing is unexcelled in adding "presence" to your outfit.

Furs. Unless you're fortunate enough to have a buffalo robe you can turn into a coat, mittens, and winter moccasins, furs are used primarily for caps, hat bands, and other decoration. They lend a real "wild and wooly" appearance to the 'skinner's outfit.

Rawhide. Depending upon the animal that produced it, rawhide varies from thin as parchment to the armor plating used in war shields. It's especially suitable for making articles that need to be stiff, like parfleches (Indian suitcases), knife sheaths, and moccasin soles. Because rawhide stretches when wet, it serves as an all-purpose, primitive fix-it material.

Canvas or cotton duck. The plain white stuff. During the time of the mountain men, canvas or sailcloth was a coarse linen, but we get by with cotton. It sees its greatest use in tents, ground cloths, and storage bags.

Trade cloth. Flannel and serge in red and navy are what most people use, along with calico. The latter isn't quite the same as the printed Calcutta cloth used during the fur trade, but it serves. Unbleached muslin is also popular when temperatures soar.

A Primitive Sewing Kit

Many 'skinners carry a kit for making repairs to clothing and equipment as routinely as they do a firesteel and flint. And although machine-stitched articles are accepted at the rendezvous, they aren't strictly authentic, as sewing machines weren't used until about 1840. Here are some of the items you'll need for hand-sewing clothing:

Artificial sinew. A heavy, waxed thread that can be split or unwound into finer strands. I recommend you buy a roll of a couple hundred yards right off the bat. Sinew is the all-purpose thread of buckskinning, used for everything from heavy-duty lacing to beadwork.

Needles. Upholstery or glover's needles top the list. Available in different sizes, they have cutting edges owing to a triangular cross section. You can use them on all but the heaviest leathers without first punching holes with an awl—and that makes their stitches more watertight.

Sailor's palm. This glove-like item works on heavy sewing like a thimble does for the light stuff. You can buy them at stores where leathercraft supplies are sold.

Rotary leather punch. A rotating rowel gives you a choice of different size holes. Great for belts; lousy for moccasins (I'll explain later). The leathercraft outfits have this, too.

Other. Awl, needlenose pliers, plastic or rawhide mallet, and Band-Aids.

Band-Aids? You betcha. Spend an evening tugging artificial sinew through stiff leather and you are certain to produce a nasty raw spot on the bottom of your little finger, where the sinew rubs each time you pull a stitch tight. You can put the Band-Aid on before, or after, your choice.

Making Moccasins

The first thing you ought to make yourself is a pair of moccasins. Then go right ahead and make about two more pairs. They wear out quickly under hard use, and it's nice to be able to rotate them in wet weather. Most of the mountain men pictured by Alfred Jacob Miller appear to be wearing a

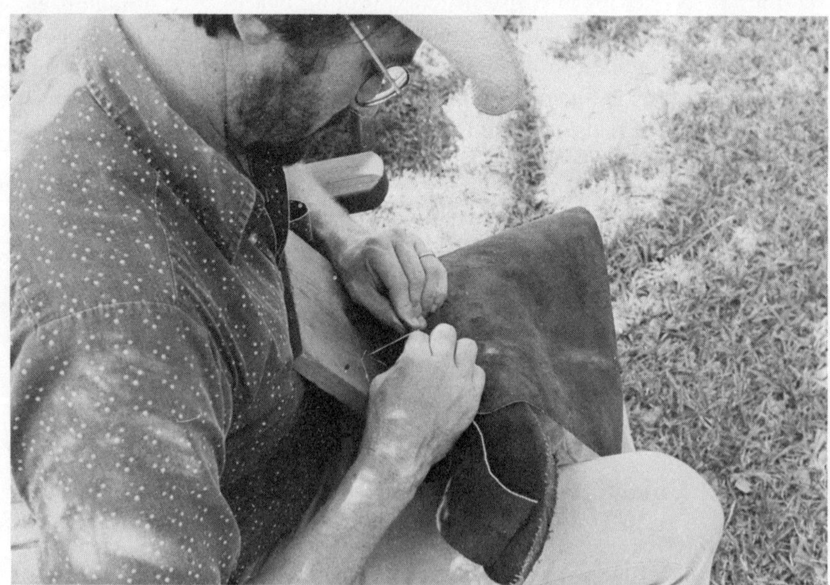

An alternative to a sailor's palm is to use a board as a thimble, as the author is doing here while sewing high tops on a pair of moccasins.

Kutenais style of soft-sole, gathered-toe moccasins. It's likely there were Kutenais at the rendezvous, and their type of footgear may have been in use among the Flatheads, whose range they shared. Mountain men never walked when they could ride, and they bundled their feet in heavy blanketing before pulling their moccasins on, so they probably got along fairly well with the soft soles.

This sketch by Alfred Jacob Miller shows the gathered-toe moccasin worn by many mountain men. The trapper on the right is sporting a beard, while the other has none. The answer to the modern-day controversy about whether mountain men wore beards seems to be that some did, and some didn't. (Courtesy of The Walters Art Gallery, Baltimore, Maryland)

The average 'skinner is far better off with a more typical plains-type, hard-sole moccasin. I've chosen an Assiniboine style because it's simple to make and is appropriate for the time and place of the mountain fur trade.

You'll need soft, tanned leather for the uppers, rawhide or stiff cowhide for the soles. Tools and other materials include an awl; scissors; sailor's palm and needlenose pliers; glover's needle and artificial sinew; tracing paper and something stiffer, like a grocery bag, for your pattern; pencil; and don't forget that Band-Aid.

Cut out the two large sides of the grocery bag, if that's what you're using. The reason I say use heavy paper instead of something like newsprint is that it will withstand the construction of several subsequent pairs of moccasins.

Stand with your foot flat on one of the sheets of heavy paper, your weight evenly distributed, and have someone draw an outline of your foot. With a measuring tape, determine how many inches it is from the floor, over your foot, and back to the floor again (Figure 8-1). Make this measurement from the forward part of your arch, over your instep, and down to the outside of your foot about where that bony projection is (the knob of the outer metatarsal bone where it links up with the cuboid, if you must know). Mark two spots on the outline of your foot corresponding to where the measurement began and ended.

Now remove your foot from the pattern. Lay the tape flat across the outline passing it across the two spots you marked. The ends of the measuring tape, equal to the distance you measured over your foot, will project past the sides of your outlined foot. Adjust the position of the tape until there is about the same amount of overlap on each side, then make a mark at each end of the tape. What you are doing here is marking off how much upper you'll have to cover that part of your foot, so don't be too cavalier about the measurement.

You now have an outline of your foot with a mark on each side about the same distance from the outline. Next, draw a straight line connecting those marks, the *instep line*.

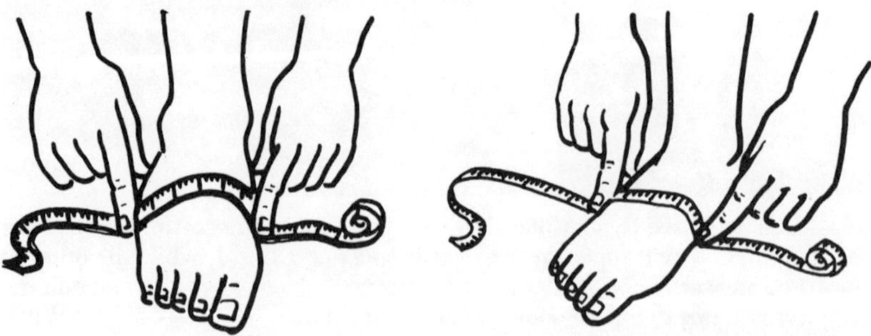

FIGURE 8–1   Making moccasins: Measuring foot for the instep line on pattern.

On the outline of your foot, mark the center of the toes and the center of the heel; then draw another line, the *center line*, connecting these.

You should now have a cross roughly through the middle of the outline. A final line, the *heel line*, is now drawn about an inch behind the heel, parallel to the instep line. This delineates the seam up the back of the moccasin. It's the last seam to be stitched, and you can then trim it some for a good fit.

Now comes the freehand stuff. Draw a line around the toes, about a half-inch beyond the outline, then extrapolate both ends through the end marks of the instep line until they intersect the heel line. You wind up with a fan-shaped pattern, which you cut out (Figure 8-2).

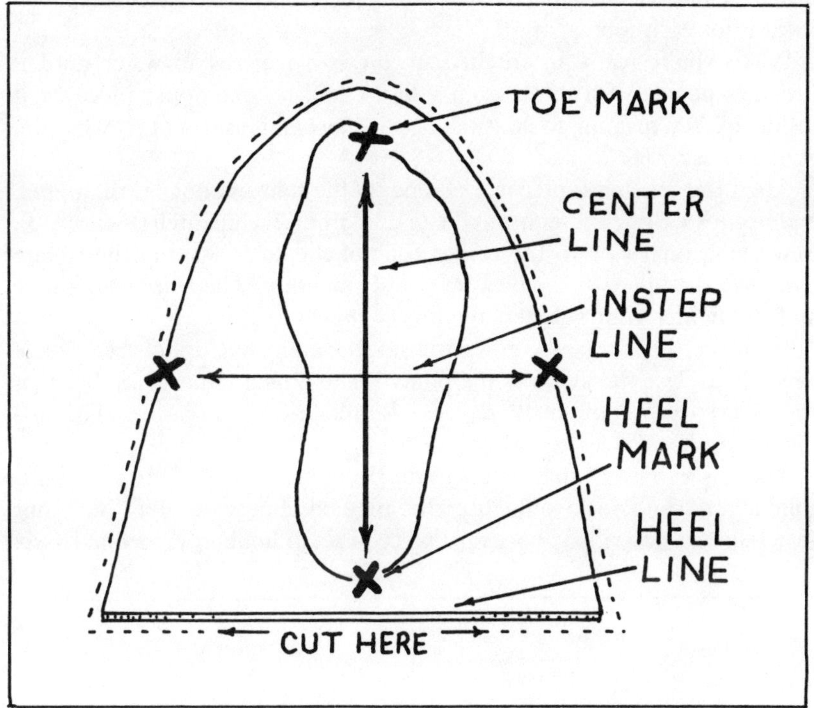

FIGURE 8–2 Making moccasins: The basic pattern for upper completed.

Make a T-shaped slit by cutting along the center line from the heel to the instep line and then along the instep line about an inch to each side of the center.

Lay the pattern on the leather and trace. Cut out the upper and transfer the toe center mark to the leather. Bear in mind which side of the leather you want showing on the finished moccasin.

If you're going to do any beadwork, now's the time. If you plan to fully bead the moccasins, you should make your upper pattern about a fourth of an inch larger all around. More about beadwork later.

Using the tracing paper, make another outline of your foot from the original pattern. This will be the pattern for the sole. Take care to duplicate the center mark for the toe—that's where you'll begin stitching sole and upper together. Lay the sole pattern on the rawhide or stiff cowhide, trace the pattern onto the sole material, and then cut out the sole. Remember to transfer the toe center mark to the sole.

To make the moccasin for the opposite foot, you can either make another pattern or flop (reverse) the one you have and hope your feet are about the same size. If your feet differ by a half size or more, or if one instep is markedly higher than the other, it's best to make a separate pattern for each foot.

When you're ready to stitch, soak the sole material in water until it becomes pliable. Turn it bottom-side up, and lay the upper piece on it inside up. You're going to be stitching the moccasin inside out, is what I'm trying to say.

Align the two toe center marks, one on the sole and one on the upper, and begin stitching there, using the in-and-around whipstitch (Figure 8-3). Sew along each side to the center back of the sole, shaping the square corner of the upper at the heel line to fit smoothly. The finer your sinew and the tighter your stitches, the longer they'll last.

In all probability, you're going to find that even a big upholstery needle needs help. Use the awl, *not* the punch. The punch removes leather that the sinew can't completely replace. Result: leaky moccasins. The awl merely pushes the leather aside.

There is a shortcut that avoids having to use an awl. Probably no right-thinking Assiniboine would use this method, but I do. Lay out your materials as I described above on a piece of scrap lumber, say a one-by-six

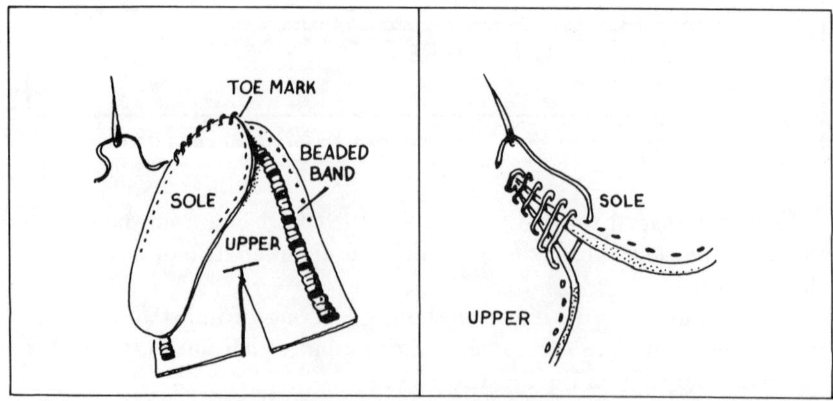

FIGURE 8–3   Making moccasins: Stitching sole to upper.

that's at least a couple of feet long. Pour out a pile of sixpenny finishing nails, the ones with the little heads, and drive the first one through both toe marks—right where you're going to take the first stitch. Nail it just far enough to secure the leather to the wood.

I say use finishing nails because you can hammer them in a row close together, and so you do, going right along the edges of the sole and upper until you have the sole outlined in nails and the upper pushed up into the form of a moccasin. When you try to pull the first nail out, both the sole and upper will likely come ripping out of the wood but the nails will remain snug in the wet leather. The only way to pull them out is to use patience and the needlenose pliers, but the result is a series of perfectly aligned holes ready for the stitching operation.

The tongue, cut from scraps left over from the uppers, can be square, rounded, or fringed on the end as well as the forked version shown in Figure 8-4. Whipstitch it to the instep line after you've turned the moccasin right-side out. Shape the back seam to fit your foot and sew it from the *inside*. Cut small slits around the top and lace in the thong for tying.

If you put on the moccasins while the soles are still wet and wear them until they are dry, you'll get an especially comfortable fit.

For moccasins that will be worn with a couple of pairs of heavy socks, you'll have to draw that initial foot outline a little larger. How *much* larger is unfortunately not subject to formulization. Take your best guess and

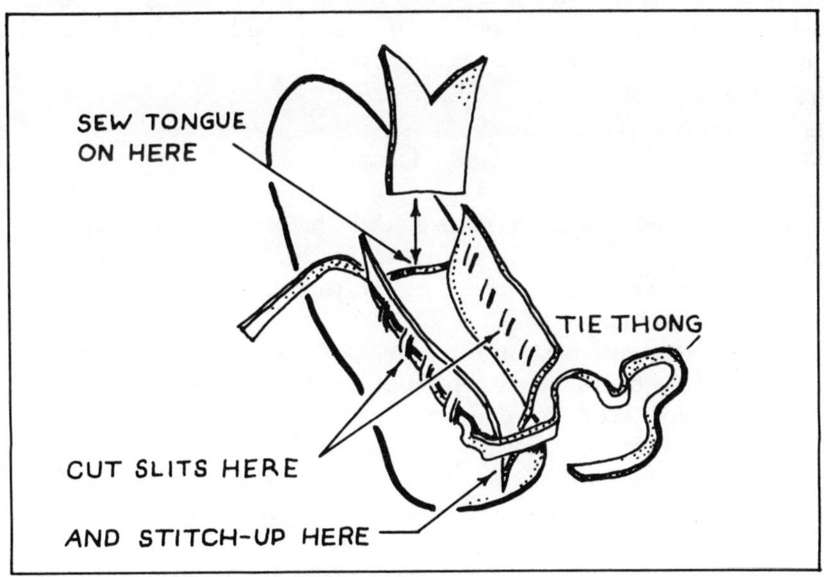

FIGURE 8–4   Making moccasins: The final steps.

until you figure it out, maybe several pairs later, let the moccasins dictate how many socks you can wear with them.

I have two pairs that are large enough for me to wear a couple of pairs of heavy wool socks and blanketing liners similar to the felt liners used in hunting boots. The liners are simply blanket moccasins, made using essentially the same procedure described above. I've tramped around in snow and mud all day long in twenty-degree weather, and although I could tell the ground was cold, my feet never became uncomfortable.

To waterproof moccasins, daub on a melted mixture of beeswax and tallow, paying special attention to seams and to the napped side of the leather, whether it's on the inside or out. It makes for a really ugly pair of moccasins, and I'm not certain you would want to do it to ones with fine beadwork—but then you probably wouldn't want to wear beaded moccasins over wet ground anyhow.

I prefer painting moccasins to beading them for decoration. It's perfectly authentic and, in the Indian way of thinking, a much more masculine undertaking. And a heck of a lot easier.

To make moccasin "boots," sew an extra piece at the top and either lace it up the front, with loops or slits for the lacing, or wrap a thong around your ankle and calf in the Flathead style. A pair of high-top moccasins really bailed me out on a long trail ride once. Wearing regular moccasins, the stirrup leathers ate into my shins until they drew blood. I switched footgear on the second day out and my troubles were over.

Incidentally, not all the mountain men's moccasins were made by Indians. Craftsmen down at Taos and thereabouts turned out a shaped-sole type that laced through holes in the upper and looked a lot like the modern shoe we call desert boots or chukkas.

Conk Covers

If moccasins are near universal in buckskinner's wardrobes, what they wear on their heads comes in profuse variety. Selecting your headgear is where you can get in character and express your individuality at the same time. And have some fun.

The commonsense move is to buy yourself a wide-brimmed buckskinner's felt hat, either the round-topped St. Louis trapper model or the flat Spanish version. While authentic, such a conk cover also has the virtue of being an excellent choice for any outdoorsman.

The top hat gets a C-minus for practicality, but an A-plus for style in my book. Beaver toppers, and later silk ones, were the mark of the discriminating dresser in the mountains as well as back in the cities. Generally, it was the traders and booshways who wore them, not the wilderness-bound trapper. Either one of these hats can be mountainized with the addition of a fur, leather, or beaded band and maybe a feather or two.

Knit liberty caps and tuques, which are like modern toboggans except not as bulky, are popular as a backup during cold weather, or as a nightcap to help conserve body heat.

Fur caps, including the visored bearskin cap which has become the mark

Wide-brimmed, round-topped felt hats are both authentic and practical. Here, members of the Texas Army reload after firing "blanks" (paper wadding over charges) during a parade to help celebrate a historical occasion.

of the free trapper, can be purchased from many of the 'skinner supply outfits. If you already have the fur, though, they're easy to make. Take an old felt hat and cut the crown free from the brim so that it fits on your head like a skullcap. It may be necessary to cut the crown above the sweatband, and in that case, sew in another one to help the cap hold its size. You can apply the fur in patches or strips if the hides are small and you're having to use several. Or position a larger hide on the crown and tack it down with stitches or ties of artificial sinew. If the head of, say, a coon has been completely skinned out, position the face at the front of the cap and let the back legs and tail drape down to shelter your neck.

A bandeau is a wide headband of fur worn by the mountain Indians, French-Canadians, and probably some American trappers as well. You might decorate it with feathers or tails. In warm weather, some 'skinners simply tie on a bandana headband or skullcap.

One of the easiest pieces of fur-trade headgear to make—and hardest to wear—is the blanket cap, a sort of hood without the parka. If you're sitting still, one of these works fine. Move around, though, and it slips down over your eyes or back off your head. Or it gets turned crosswise where you can't see. The only way I can see how the trappers could have worn these things (and it seems plausible, based on what we know about personal hygiene in the mountains) is that their hair was so greasy that the cap was plastered into place. Blanket caps commonly had twin "wolf ear" peaks on top and were decorated with feathers. (See Figure 8-5).

The Hunting Shirt

The buckskin hunting shirt or jacket, in a variety of styles, is a universal favorite among 'skinners. The traditional longhunter's fringed hunting shirt and the crudely fashioned, poncho-like Indian war shirt are probably the two most popular.

Strictly speaking, the eastern hunting shirt is more correct, even for the Western Fur Trade Era. While the mountain men did obtain clothing from the Indians, they were most likely to be tailored in the white man's fashion, some of them in pretty *high* fashion. Beadwork was usually in the floral applique of the East rather than the crude geometric patterns of the plains. The increasing influence from the southern Rockies was shown in the late-period popularity of the waist-length New Mexican riding jacket.

Patterns for the traditional hunting shirt are available from many of the merchants listed in Chapter 7. As for the war shirt, the hides you use pretty much determine the pattern.

In a typical war shirt (Figure 8-6), the bottom part of the tunic is left natural, with legs dangling. False legs were sometimes stitched on to heighten this "natural" effect. The shirt is stitched at the shoulders and the

Flat-topped, Spanish-style felt hats are worn by figures on the right in this Alfred Jacob Miller painting. The central figure is wearing a blanket cap, easy to make but nearly impossible for modern 'skinners to wear according to the author. (Courtesy of The Walters Art Gallery, Baltimore, Maryland)

simple crew neck is adorned front and back with triangle-shaped bibs, which are beaded or decorated with wool or trade cloth. The sleeves are sewn from the wrist to the elbow and the upper parts are left in natural contours, closed under the arms by lacing. Sides are laced also.

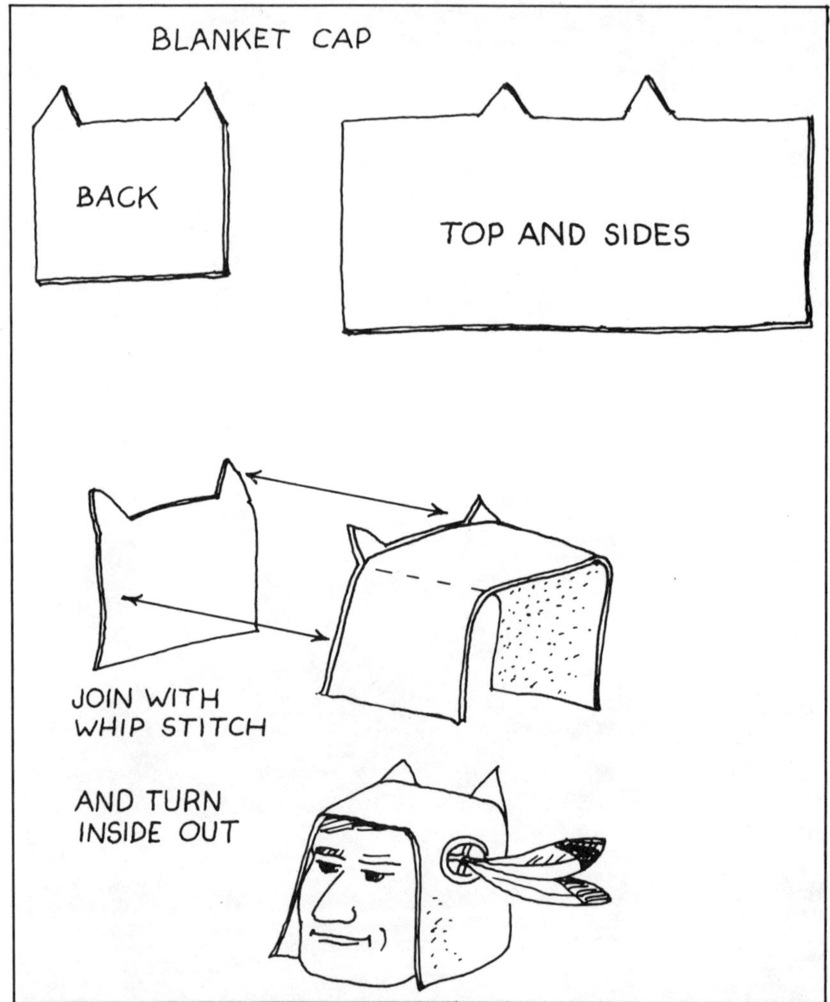

FIGURE 8–5   Making a blanket cap.

All the free edges at cuffs and tails are cut in shallow fringe, less than half an inch. Wide bands of quillwork or lazy-squaw beading loop over both shoulders and down the back and chest. Ermine tails, tin cones, or bogus scalps of horsehair hang from the front.

The war shirt is a pretty impressive article of clothing and I can't blame 'skinners for adopting it in the face of historical evidence to the contrary.

For warm weather or for those times when you need a "work" costume and you don't want to mess up your buckskin finery, a simple pullover shirt of calico, flannel, muslin, or serge is just the thing. Here again you can buy patterns, or finished shirts, of authentic nineteenth-century styles

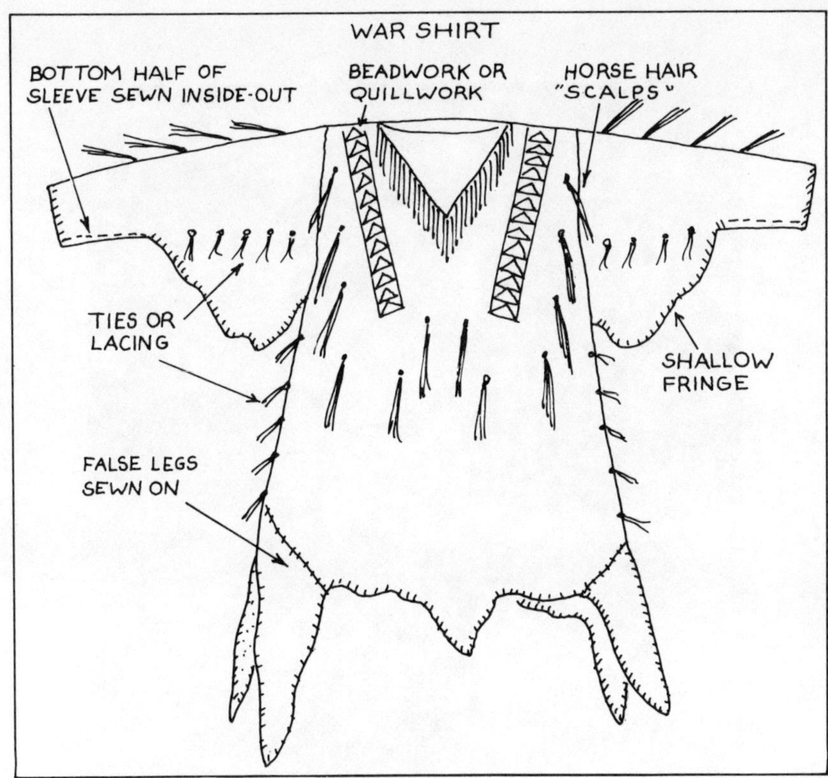

FIGURE 8–6   Design of a typical war shirt.

with puffy sleeves and gathers under the yoke. Or you can throw something together using a modern shirt as a guide. Make it simple and red and you can't go wrong.

Breeches, Leggings, Capotes, and Mittens

Generally speaking, breeches should be high-waisted and snug-fitting. Take your choice of single, buttoned fly, or drop front like the navyman's traditional thirteen-button trousers. Buttoned suspenders, or galluses, were common, but belt loops were not unknown. Buckskin pants usually have fringe and sometimes a beaded or quillwork band up each side seam.

The most comfortable, serviceable pair of pants I own, primitive or otherwise, is a pair I made of wool blanketing using an old pair of Levis as a pattern. Not wanting to use a zipper, of course, I changed the fly so it would overlap and button, and I added a high waistband.

As I mentioned earlier, a lot of 'skinners are going to breechclout and

In his St. Louis trapper hat and calico shirt, this *hiverano* is sensibly attired for mild weather. To get that real mountain man look, with fur caps and heavy skins, you need real mountain man weather.

leggins, claiming they've never known such comfort. I don't know about that, but a pair of buckskin or even canvas leggings worn over your trousers would be nice for added warmth in cold weather and protection on horseback.

Buckskin leggings are nothing more than pants legs with a thong or wider piece that comes up to the waist and attaches to the belt. They are usually fringed at the outside seam and sometimes beaded or quilled just ahead of it. Indian blanket leggings are rectangular pieces folded over and sewn on a diagonal so the opening at the top is wide enough for the thigh and that at the bottom allows the foot to slip through. The excess material is left to flop like batwing chaps. They're usually trimmed in trade cloth of a contrasting color and other decorations such as tin cones or beadwork may be added. A strap of wool or leather secures each legging to the belt.

In really hot weather like we get down here in Texas, a fellow in clothing designed for the Rocky Mountains is going to do some sweltering. In colder climes, however, primitive garb really shines. I spent a week hunting in the Adirondacks one October when the temperature dropped into the twenties and it rained or snowed every blessed day. I tried both modern clothing and primitive, and I can say without hesitation that I stayed more comfortable in my wool trousers and capote than I did in insulated coveralls and rubberized raingear.

A capote is a French-Canadian blanket coat—an overcoat with a hood, really—that was very popular with the mountain men. Many 'skinners still make them out of Hudson's Bay point blankets, but that's too rich for my blood. I made mine from a pair of gray army surplus blankets. I left off the fringe at the shoulders, which was apparently in vogue after the mountain fur trade years (although it's certainly the fashion now), and added the big patch pockets on the side which I had seen in a Miller sketch. I also installed a double row of buttons as in the sketch. Many 'skinners simply close their capotes by wrapping them around and tying on a sash.

The two long tails of blanketing hanging from the hood of a capote may seem like useless decoration, but they're designed to wrap around your neck like a muffler.

Mittens are easy to make. Lay your hand palm up on a piece of paper with your fingers together and thumb folded over on your palm. Draw an outline, a little larger than life, that includes a reasonable portion of your wrist. No need to be fancy; it ought to be little more than an inverted U. That's the pattern for the backside of the mitten (A), shown in Figure 8-7.

Now make a duplicate of A, cut away the curved portion corresponding to the base of the thumb, and you have the palm (B).

Make a pattern of your thumb, just a simple little inverted U but extend it on down at the bottom so the material will reach the wrist. Make two of them, one for the print side (C) and one for the nail side (D).

These patterns will work well on blanketing and rabbit skins. But you

The fellow with the feather in his hat is wearing a typical capote, made with a four-point Hudson's Bay blanket (note the four bars in the front above the broad lower stripe). The capote, of Canadian origin, became widely accepted in the Rockies during the fur trade. The other guy is wearing a homespun eastern rifleman's coat. (Photo by Gene Hyre)

should enlarge them a little if you transfer them to something with a lot of pile to it, like sheepskin or buffalo hide, if you're going to put the shaggy side in. Also, with hides or skins, remember to reverse each pattern when you transfer it a second time so you wind up with a left and a right mitten.

To assemble each mitten, join B to C along the base of the thumb; join A to B from the thumb, over the fingers and down to the wrist (keep the stitching along the thumb line between parts B and C to the outside since you'll be turning the mitten inside out when you're finished); finally, join D to A and C.

These mittens are crude, but they have the virtue of being easily shaken off if you need bare hands in a hurry—to bushwack a whitetail, say. An "idiot string" from one mitten to the other running through the sleeves of your capote will prevent you from losing them in the thrill of the chase.

With the clothing described in this chapter, you'll be "up to Green River," and a sterling example to the wave of pork-eaters coming after you.

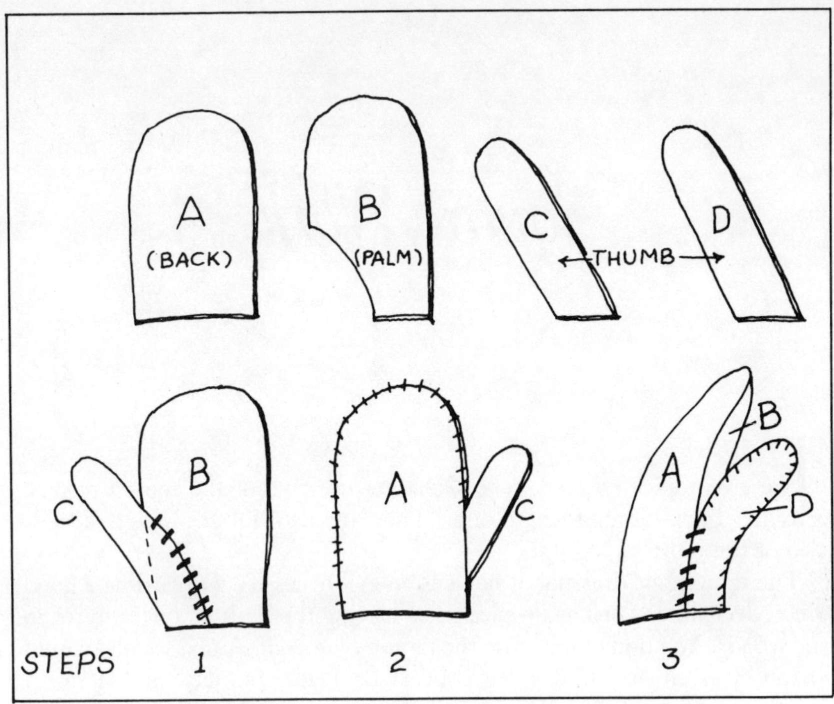

FIGURE 8–7   Making mittens: *top*, pattern pieces; *bottom*, assembly steps.

9

Squaw Work

The two topics covered in this chapter are two of the most tiresome activities buckskinning has to offer. They are also, I'll grudgingly admit, two of the most satisfying.

The tanning or dressing of hides is an evil necessity. Discarding a good green deer hide is just as despicable as leaving the flesh of a deer to rot in the woods. You don't have to do the tanning yourself. A taxidermist would charge you an arm and a leg, but W.B. Place Tannery in Hartford, Wisconsin, tans deer hides for $10 to $20 per hide, depending upon whether you want the hair left on or not. However, it does take quite a while to get your hides back. And if you want genuine brain-tanned skins, Indian-style, then you *are* going to have to take on the job yourself.

Unless you're a woman, there's no excuse for doing your own beadwork. I know I must sound like a raging male chauvinist porker here, but historians will bear me out. Beading and quillwork, and for that matter tanning, were squaw work. Painting and war were the male art forms.

Oh, I suppose I can concede that a hairy-chested mountain man might take on a little applique with beads or porcupine quills in the dead of winter while he was holed up in some dugout, bored out of his mind. And trappers frequently had to do their own fleshing, stretching, and pressing of beaver plews, so the preparation of a buffalo or elk hide certainly wouldn't be beneath him.

I'm not saying it was never done—just that it was never done cheerfully.

There are plenty of sources of finished beadwork. The popularity of buckskinning has spawned a huge cottage industry of folks sitting hunched over saucers of loose beads, decorating moccasins and making rosettes and bands. Their wares are sold through some of the dealers listed in Chapter 7 and on trade blankets at the major rendezvous.

However. Beadwork is expensive. You can seldom order exactly what you want in terms of colors and designs. And that goes double or more for

Squaw work is usually taken to mean menial and disagreeable tasks, but if you can do the work of one-half squaw, you're doing something. Besides the tedious jobs— like the seam-stitching these women are doing—squaws used to do really backbreaking work like dressing hides and moving camp.

quillwork. I'm afraid it's down to this again: If you want it done right (i.e., the way *you* want it), you have to do it yourself.

Brain-Tanning Hides

Tanning a hide begins when you're skinning the animal. Take your time. It's a lot easier to peel that fat, flesh and gristle off when some of it is still attached to the carcass. Shave it back from the skin as you go, and go *slow!*

When the hide is off and most of the flesh and fat removed, lay it hair-side down, stretch it out as best you can, and dump salt on it. Be prepared to use from five to ten pounds, enough to thoroughly salt every inch of the flesh side. And use table salt. I don't know why, but a lot of folks seem to have the idea that you use rock salt to preserve hides. It *would* work—after you got out a ball-peen hammer and pounded it all down to the fineness of table salt.

Assuming you're at a deer camp someplace and will have to put the hide aside until you can get home and find the time to work on it, storage is your next problem. Forget plastic bags, they hold heat and will cause even a well-salted hide to rot. (What the salt is doing is sucking the moisture out, but a plastic bag will trap moisture.) Instead, roll the hide loosely and put it in a gunny sack or some similar container that will keep the flies off but allow some air circulation.

Most Indians preferred to make clothing from the skins of animals killed in the summer. Not only were the skins thinner and more suitable, but the weather was more conducive to the job at hand. Buckskinners often have to do their tanning in the winter, when spells of bad weather are likely to cause a halt in the process. Storage can really be a problem then. When several days in a row of good weather are forecast, it's best to set aside enough time to complete the tanning job.

When you're ready to work on the hide, soak the salt-cured hide in a big plastic garbage can overnight. Because deer hair is hollow, the hide will float. Weight it down well with rocks or whatever. Drain and replace the water at least twice during this soaking stage.

When the hide is pliable, almost like green again, you must flesh it. You may think you did that when you skinned the deer. But, you've got to scrape down to the bluish-white skin, and at the very least there's a membrane still in the way.

Fleshing is best done with the hide stretched in a frame. The old Indian way was to fashion a square frame of stout poles and lace the hide across the center of it with rawhide thongs. I do essentially the same thing, nailing two-by-twos together and using nylon cord for lacing. A sharp, thin-bladed knife like those used for filleting fish makes the best openings

Michael "Two Bears" Hughes uses a lodge pole and an ax handle to wring out a skin before stretching it.

for weaving the cord through the edge of the hide. You need a slit; a hole, such as that made by an ice pick or an awl, just doesn't give you enough to work with. The slits can be about three inches apart along the sides, but they need to be closer, up to an inch apart, at the ends of the legs and in the neck and tail areas.

Michael "Two Bears" Hughes, a guy who tans a lot of hides during the course of a year, has devised a stretching technique that is much quicker than the traditional lacing method. All around a two-by-four frame, he nailed ten-penny nails, spacing them a couple of inches apart and letting them stick out an inch or so. With a wire cutter, he clipped the heads off. He cut old leather belts into lengths of between eight inches and two feet and then fastened hooks formed of bent and sharpened eight-penny nails at one end. To stretch a skin, Two Bears snags the hide with the hooks and pulls on the belts, fitting the belt holes over the nails in the frame. The tension on the skin is easily adjusted by moving the belts from one hole to another.

You can buy a special fleshing tool, which looks like a small double-bladed hoe, from firms that supply trapping tools. A copy of *Fur-Fish-Game* magazine would yield the names of some of these outfits. I'm happy with a common paint scraper sharpened with a small mill file. I did have to round off the ends of the blade so they wouldn't gouge the hide; it took me several nice nicks to figure that out.

Two Bears' stretching frame has old belts with bent-nail hooks to grab the skin. The belts are looped over nails in the frame. A skin can be stretched much faster by this method than by the traditional lacing method.

The two tools on the left are used for fleshing hides by professional trappers. The straight razor *(center)* is useful for scraping hard-to-reach areas around the edge of a skin. The two scrapers on the right are homemade, the larger one having a blade from a carpenter's plane.

If you want a robe—a tanned hide with the hair left on it—you can skip the next process, and count yourself lucky. Dehairing can really be tedious, depending upon how powerful your particular medicine is in causing the hair to slip without rotting the skin.

Actually, deerskin robes are nice to have around. The hollow hairs make pretty fair insulation. Flop a few robes down on the floor of your lean-to and lay your bedroll on top and you'll be toasty.

Sooner or later, though, you are going to want buckskin for clothing or articles like pipe bags. We might as well get to it.

Theoretically, a couple days more of soaking, changing the water at least once a day, will finally cause the hair to slip and make it easy to remove. The one time I tried it that way, I would up practically lathering the damn thing and shaving it! Since then I've leaned heavily toward the method of using natural lye from hardwood ashes to speed up the dehairing process. Build a fire of wood such as hickory or oak, make a paste of the ashes with water, and work it thoroughly into the hair. Then soak the hide in a solution of water and more ashes in a small container, just large enough to keep the roll or bundled hide submerged. This time, don't change the water. But once or twice a day, check to see if the hair is slipping. When it starts coming out freely at the shoulder, where the hair is the thickest, you should be able to pluck it like a duck.

No cause for celebration yet, however; the work is far from over!

To wind up with true Indian-style buckskin with a nap, or sueded finish, on both sides, you must scrape the thin epidermis off the hair side. You can either stretch the hide back in your frame or drape it over a beaming board and rake it over with an edged tool, or you can work it like a shoeshine rag over a "beam"—a wooden blade set in the ground or fixed to a bench.

The beaming board looks like a big ironing board set in the ground at a forty-five-degree angle. The surface is smooth and slightly rounded. You lay the hide flesh-side down and scrape the hair side with a double-handled beaming tool, available where they sell trapping supplies. The beaming board is designed for use with case-skinned animals—where the skin is slit hind foot to hind foot then peeled back off the animal in a tube, which is then fit over the end of the board. To work a deer hide on the beaming board is a two-squaw job; one person to hold the hide in place while the other scrapes.

I use the frame myself, and as a scraper, a cheap kitchen "scalper" with plenty of flex in the blade. With any edged tool at this point you must concentrate on moving the blade perpendicular to the cutting edge. Even a slight sideways motion is apt to cut into the skin. The bow in the blade of my scalper helps to minimize the danger.

Once you get the remaining hair and the epidermis removed, set the hide aside and let it dry. What you have now is Indian rawhide, and every fourth hide or so you may want to stop right there. The stuff has a thousand uses in buckskinning, especially when it comes from the thick skin of an old buck.

Nah, you want a war shirt, right? Very well, let's get on with it.

Soak the hide once more, just until it's soft and pliable. Lace it back into the frame and stretch it tight. Cook up a mush of two pork brains in about a quart of water. When it's grayish-white and about the consistency of cooked oatmeal, it's ready. (You can buy the brains at the meat market. The Indians frequently used the brain of the animal that also previously owned the hide, and the old rule of thumb was that every animal had just enough brains to tan itself. Sometimes the Indians preserved cakes of dried brains mixed with grass or moss for later use. You can do what you want, but I'm going to the butcher shop for mine.)

Rub the mush in on both sides of the hide, or just on the flesh side if you're tanning a robe. Let it stand overnight.

The brains leave a fatty substance in the fiber of the skin very much like neat's-foot oil. In fact, you can *use* neat's-foot oil if you want to cheat. But the transition of stiff rawhide into supple buckskin is largely accomplished by a mechanical process of breaking and stretching the fibers. Begin by using a blunt tool—the handle of a wooden canoe paddle works fine—to flex the hide. Tighten the lacing as required and keep kneading both sides,

Phil "No Kill" Wood demonstrates the use of the beaming board. With a case-skinned animal, like the raccoon he is working on, it takes just one person to use the board. With a flat hide like that of a deer, it would take a second person to hold the hide in place.

The author uses a common kitchen knife, or "scalper," to dehair buckskin. Not only the hair, but the outer layer of skin must be removed to obtain the sueded finish on both sides common to brain-tanned hides. The hide is stretched across the same frame the author uses while fleshing it.

covering every inch, until most of the remaining moisture is wrung out. And if it's easy for you, you aren't doing it right.

When there's only a little dampness left in the hide, unlace it and trim the edges. Loop it around a small tree or a stake and twist it, using something like a tomahawk handle for extra leverage to really wring it out.

Now the work begins: You need a taut rope, a half-inch or more in diameter, running vertically. The usual procedure is to tie one end of the rope securely to the trunk of a tree, near the ground, and the other to an overhead limb. Pass the hide between the rope and the tree, grasp the ends as though you were going to pop a towel, and work the hide back and forth across the rope, pulling tight and changing your grip on the hide so as to stretch it all around. The more you stretch the hide and rub it against the rope, the softer and thicker it will be.

Once you finish that stage to your satisfaction, you will have the creamy buckskin the Indians used for ceremonial dress. But if it gets wet, it'll stiffen up and will have to reworked. Smoking is used to make Indian-

The Plains Indians used rawhide, or dry untanned skin, for many purposes. It was called *parflech* by the French traders because shields made of thick buffalo rawhide could deflect arrows. Eventually the word was applied to the beautifully crafted Indian "suitcases" made of the material. The woman in this painting by Olaf C. Seltzer is using a fleshing tool to scuff, or whiten, rawhide for an attractive texture. (Courtesy of The Thomas Gilcrease Institute of American History and Art, Tulsa, Oklahoma)

tanned skins water-resistant and to give them the buckskin color. Indians used the tops of discarded lodge covers, which had been constantly smoked for a year or more, to make moccasins and leggings.

Sew the hide into a cone or funnel shape—a miniature tipi, you could say. Dig a hole at least two feet deep and almost—but not quite—large enough in diameter to use up the "floor" area of the hide tipi. Then burrow a small tunnel into the side of the hole, starting at ground level about a yard's distance from the hole (see Figure 9-1). You may have to use a plastic pipe to keep the tunnel from collapsing. Build a smudge fire in the hole using briquettes for the backyard barbecue to which is added punky wood from a rotten log. Now suspend the "tipi" by means of a tripod or

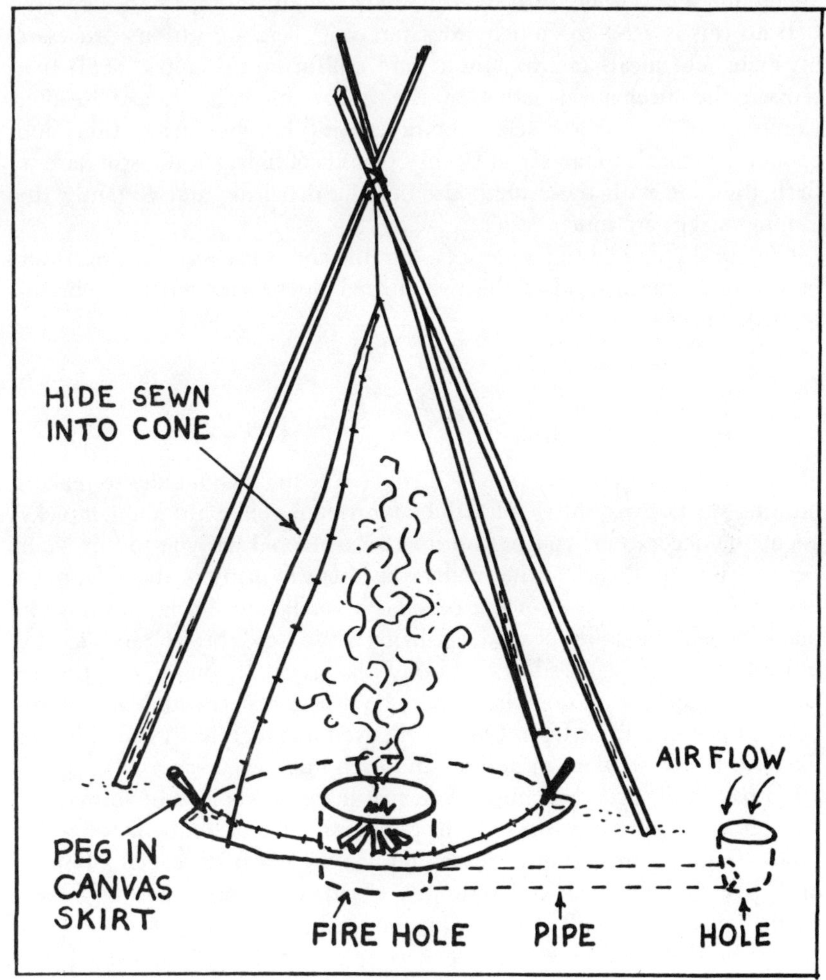

FIGURE 9–1 "Tipi" method for smoking a hide.

overhanging limb directly over the fire. You may want to sew a margin of canvas around the bottom to peg the "tipi" around the hole. Air coming in through the tunnel will keep the fire going, with the smoke billowing out of the top of the hide funnel. It may be necessary to prop the funnel open with a cross of green sticks placed inside.

You have to watch this operation closely—one lick of flame and a portion of buckskin is ruined—and it's a lengthy operation. The hide should be smoked for several hours at least.

The color of the skin will progress from a light tan through bright orange to a dark chestnut as it smokes. You can stop at any point the color pleases you, but the longer you smoke it, the better it will shed water. When one side is done, turn the funnel inside out and repeat the process.

If all this is a bit too much work for you, there are various processes involving chemicals (alum, tannic acid, sulfuric acid, nitric acid) that replace the mechanical action of the Indian method. Tandy Leather Company of Fort Worth sells a home tanning kit with instructions and enough chemicals to tan about twenty pounds of hides. You'll still have to flesh the hide with these methods, but the dehairing and certainly the tanning stages are much easier.

Chemically tanned hides are soft, durable and water resistant, but they have a slick side instead of the two sueded sides characteristic of brain-tanned skins.

Beadwork

Once you have laboriously provided yourself with enough hides to make a hunting shirt or war shirt, you will be forgiven if you're just a touch picky about the decorations you put on it. I wish I could tell you to buy your beadwork or quillwork at the rendezvous the way many of the old-timers did, but the fact is most of the beadwork you'll find displayed on trade blankets will be loom-beaded, utilizing little seed beads, and in the intricate and multi-colored Reservation Period style. If you can find proper lazy squaw beadwork done in simple, bold patterns with the large pony beads, the cost will be high. Quillwork, even if authentically done, is still likely to be too modern in design, and even more expensive.

To have authentic decoration, you may have no choice but to make it yourself. If you're like me, you'll swear off after every bout with the beads—only to find necessity dragging you back. I first beaded a border on a pair of moccasins and promptly decided I didn't want any more beaded moccasins (still don't). The mountain man's moccasins weren't always beaded—they may, in fact, have seldom been beaded—and I was ready to go for a little painless authenticity for a change.

Later on, however, I just *had* to have some beaded strips for my war shirt (just had to have a war shirt, too, against all reason). I couldn't find anything already beaded that suited me and couldn't afford to hire it done, so there was no way out for me. I broke out the needle and sinew and went to work. The results, black triangles or "arrow heads" on a red background, continue to be a source of great satisfaction to me. It was worth it.

Still later, after I acquired what I consider to be legitimate and serious medicine and needed a proper bag to contain it, I did some more beadwork. There may be no end to it ... which should give you fair warning.

To begin, let's assume you're going to bead some strips for the sides of your buckskin breeches or leggings. You can do it right on the article or on another piece of buckskin, light wool, flannel, or some other true-to-the-period material. Beadwork was sometimes done on a separate piece in the old days, either to make the job easier or to preserve beadwork from a worn-out article. The beaded strip is sewn in place on the garment.

Let's assume also that you're going to use a geometric design (we'll get into floral applique shortly) in the lazy squaw stitch. There are books (for example, *Crow Indian Beadwork: A Descriptive and Historical Study*, by William Wildschut and John C. Ewers) that will give you ideas on patterns and colors. Trips to museums would be helpful, too, as long as you keep in mind that you're looking for artifacts from the time period and tribes pertinent to the Western Fur Trade Era.

Don't feel you must copy existing designs to the bead, however. Be creative, within the general style. Stick with the basic colors: red, white, yellow, black, and blue. And keep it simple, which makes the planning and execution of a piece of beadwork less of a headache anyhow.

With lazy squaw beading, you lay the design down in lines of five to nine beads at a time. You can use different colors within a single line—doing so progressively to create a diagonal design, for instance—but you must keep the basic unit in mind when planning your pattern.

Try using graph paper to plan your design, with each little square representing a single bead (Figure 9-2, left). Color or shade in the squares to create your design, then outline each line of, say, five beads in the lazy squaw stitch. That way you'll know that when you get to a certain point, you're going to have to use, for example, three black ones and two reds or whatever. You may have to sketch it out several times to get it right, but that's better than having to bead something several times.

It helps to anchor the article or material you're beading—or at least the portion of it you're working on—in some sort of frame like an embroidery hoop. The idea is to keep the material in place without stretching it, because your finished beadwork might pucker or bunch up when the material relaxes again.

Knot your thread and bring the needle up through the material in the lower left-hand corner of the design (Figure 9-2, right). Pick up the

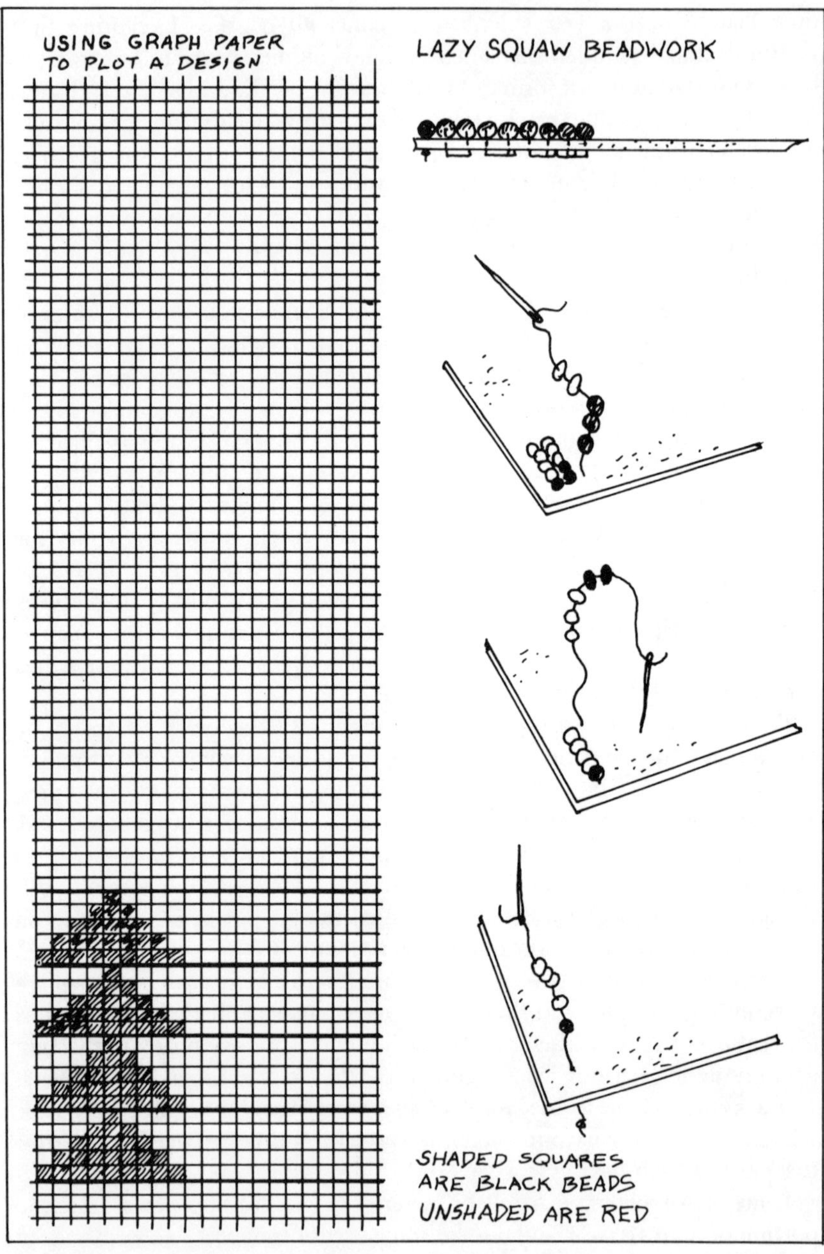

FIGURE 9–2   Lazy squaw beadwork. Use graph paper to lay out the design. Form the stitches as shown on the right.

appropriate number and color of beads, in the appropriate order, and make a stitch downrange. Bring the needle back through the material about a bead's width from where it went in, again stack on the appropriate beads, and bring a stitch back toward you. Keep going up and back like that until you finish the bottom line or bar of lazy squaw stitch. Then you start at the lower right of the next bar and work to the left.

If you keep a working number of beads in a saucer or shallow ashtray, they're easy to chase down and pick up with the point of the needle.

Beading on the soft brain-tanned skins, Indian women didn't push their needles all the way through the way I'm suggesting. Instead, they grabbed a bite about halfway through the skin with each stitch. I suspect they did this so the sinew or whatever thread they were using wouldn't rot through on the inside of the article and spill off part of the design. With artificial sinew, you and I don't have to worry about that. But if you want to be authentic inside and out, by all means go ahead.

One problem I have encountered is that beads of different colors tend to also be slightly different in size, which can throw your design out of kilter. I have compensated by adding a bead here and dropping one there when it seemed necessary. I'm sure the average squaw wasn't above a little cheating to make things come out right.

Other Methods

The floral designs put on in the free-flowing applique method, which we associate with the eastern or woodland Indians, was actually the most common type of beadwork found on the tailored buckskins of the Canadian and American mountain men. Applique is also the method used in beading the rosettes which look so good on a blanket vest or fur cap.

In floral beading, you basically string beads on a thread, arrange the thread in the pattern you want, and tack it down by looping stitches over it with another needle and thread. It sounds simple, but it's a real art form. Lazy squaw is a paint-by-numbers operation in comparison.

Rosettes are formed by tacking down concentric rings of beads, starting with a single bead in the middle. Draw your pattern directly on the material and use it to tell you which beads to string when. Say, for example, that you have a simple cross, straight lines of blue radiating from the center on a background of white. You're going to have to string more and more white beads between the blue ones as the circle grows wider, right? Sure, that's predictable, but unlike with lazy squaw, you can't predict how many of a given color will fit into a given pattern. You just string them on and lay them down. Whup! That one should have been blue. So take the white one off and put the blue one on, and if the ring looks right then, tack it down. It can get much more complicated, but you get the idea.

Though typical of the eastern or woodland Indians, floral beading like this was also common on the decorated buckskins of Canadian and American mountain men. (Photo by John Wootters)

The quillwork that antedated the introduction of trade beads and set the style for much of the beadwork is a form of embroidery using moisture-softened porcupine quills, or sometimes the stripped quills of feathers. It's done by sewing the quills down, folding them in various ways as you go to create the banded effect that the lazy squaw stitch would later mimic. Basic designs were achieved by dying quills with natural substances such as clays, ashes, and extracts of roots. For a detailed description of the basic stitches, see *The Technique of Porcupine Quill Decoration Among the Indians of North America*, by William C. Orchard.

10

The Primitive Camp

There comes a time, Pilgrim, when you must go beyond masquerading as a mountain man and start living like one—for short periods of time, anyway. Your heart won't let you do otherwise. You will have grown tired of marching back to the modern camp, you and the other newcomers separating into suddenly sullen groups that seem strange within earshot of the obvious camaraderie in the primitive camp.

Primitive camp—the very words challenge you. Oh sure, you can get along in the woods a couple of nights with old-timey gear. But will you *like* it? You hope you will because you like the idea of it: uncluttered and close to nature.

When you first sit down and take stock of what you will need for even a weekend of primitive camping, you are in for a shock. Practically nothing you use as a modern camper will suffice; you are up against the task of duplicating all of it in nineteenth-century equipment.

But, as when you first entertained the idea of dressing like a mountain man, the obstacle looms larger than it actually is. For one thing, the equipment of the early 1800s is cheaper, piece for piece, than the stuff most people use today. And there's less of it. Soon, if you're like me, you will start replacing much of your modern gear with your buckskinning gear on non-primitive outings, simply because it's both functional and aesthetic. You only have to spend an evening of conversation in the mellow, dancing light of a candle lantern to learn what aesthetic advantage that cheap and extremely portable item has over a roaring gasoline lantern.

But I'm getting ahead of myself; let's get you into the water, or camp, a toe at a time.

Just Visiting

Suppose you only want to stay over for a meal in the primitive camp. What do you need? Well, you ought to have something to eat with and out of.

Borrowing a copious and cheerful sense of hospitality from the Indians, 'skinners think nothing of drop-in guests for dinner. Meals are frequently such that they can be distributed among three, four, or a half-dozen people with the same ease, albeit not in the same proportions. When you only have three T-bones, you have a problem if a fourth diner shows up. Stew, on the other hand, can be divided by the thimbleful. But it is considered thoughtful and proper to bring your own eating utensils if you drop in for a meal.

That's not to say you need to walk around camp with a tin plate in one hand and a fork in the other like a beggar. Many 'skinners stroll about with big "tin" or enamel cups ("tin," or sheet steel, is authentic; enamel serves) dangling from their belts and soup spoons tucked inside their pipe bags or hunting pouches. Thus equipped, many a single 'skinner attends weekend rendezvous without bringing a bite of food, knowing he'll be invited to more family cookouts than he has room for in his belly. (Of course, it sometimes helps if he has a jug of some sort dangling next to his cup. The invites tend to come quicker.)

You can still buy "tin" cups in many places. The buckskinner supply houses sell both the small size and the big two-pinter which doubles as a coffee or stew pot when you do your own cooking. Handcrafted flatware is a popular item on most rendezvous trade blankets. It sure looks primitive, but most of it is pretty clumsy in actual use. Flea markets and the bargain-basement antique shops we used to call junk stores, before old junk became so popular, are good places to pick up original nineteenth-century flatware like three-tined forks and matching sets with bone or wooden handles.

You might as well start fetching around for some bedding, too. So many 'skinners today have spacious lodges—what the Dakotas have taught us to call tipis—that the "hotel space" at even a medium-size rendezvous would rival a convention center. Veteran 'skinners are proud of their lodges and furnishings and more than tickled, usually, to put up guests. If they didn't want to mingle, they wouldn't come to the rendezvous.

"Hello, the Lodge!"

Since you're certain to be invited into a lodge, either to eat, spend the night, or just palaver, you should learn a little tipi etiquette before getting any deeper into the rendezvous scene.

During their free days on the plains, Indians were highly spiritual and their lodges were temples as well as homes. The highly functional form of the tipi became symbolic as well, with the lofty tip of the cone representing the heavens, the lodge poles representing paths of communion with the Great Spirit, and so on.

Today's buckskinners adhere to that old religiosity maybe a good deal

Although its long poles make it difficult to transport in modern vehicles, the tipi is without question the most efficient portable shelter ever devised.

more than the old mountain man did. They may be good Catholics, Baptists, Methodists *et al* in everyday life, but while living in the lodge they at least go through the respectful motions evolved over centuries of year-round tipi living, especially when they have guests to impress. I don't think you and I need to get into a philosophical discussion of the validity of Indian religious beliefs at this point. The fact remains that knowing and practicing tipi etiquette is part of the fun of buckskinning.

In theory, when a lodge door is open, you're free to just step in. When it's closed, you should rap on a lodge pole or cry out "Hello, the lodge!" or "Hey, there!" or something to let the folks inside know you're outside and want to come in. In practice, you ought to make your presence known even when the door is open. When crossed sticks are tied over a closed door flap, it means nobody's home and the tipi is "locked"—a precaution that works as well at most rendezvous as burglar bars do in town.

Indian lodges were traditionally erected with the door facing east. The lodge is actually a tilted cone, with the back, or western, side forming a steeper angle than the front. Since bad weather usually comes from the west on the plains, this configuration makes the tipi an extremely strong tent in a blow. Besides, it just makes sense to face the doorway and smoke hole (also in the front of the tipi) away from rain-bearing winds. 'Skinners don't always practice this, but for the sake of orientation, let's assume the lodge owner you're visiting does.

Upon entering a tipi, a man should turn to his right, or to the north (Figure 10-1). The guest of honor is usually seated on the western side of the tipi, to the left, or "heart side," of the lodge owner. Sit wherever you're told, of course, but try not to pass between others and the centrally located fire. Walk behind them if possible, or beg their pardon profusely if there's no way past other than between them and the fire.

Women file to the south, turning left upon entering. It's indicative of the role of the Indian woman that firewood was traditionally stored on the left just inside the door. Women not only kept the fire going, they made the lodge and its furnishings and were in charge of putting it up and taking it down. The only thing a man might do is paint his war record on the liner or cover. In reality, the Indian woman was master of her lodge. But she had the good sense to let her husband lord it over her, especially when guests were present. The ladies of buckskinning are frequently no different.

You usually take what's offered you, be it a piece of meat from a bowl or

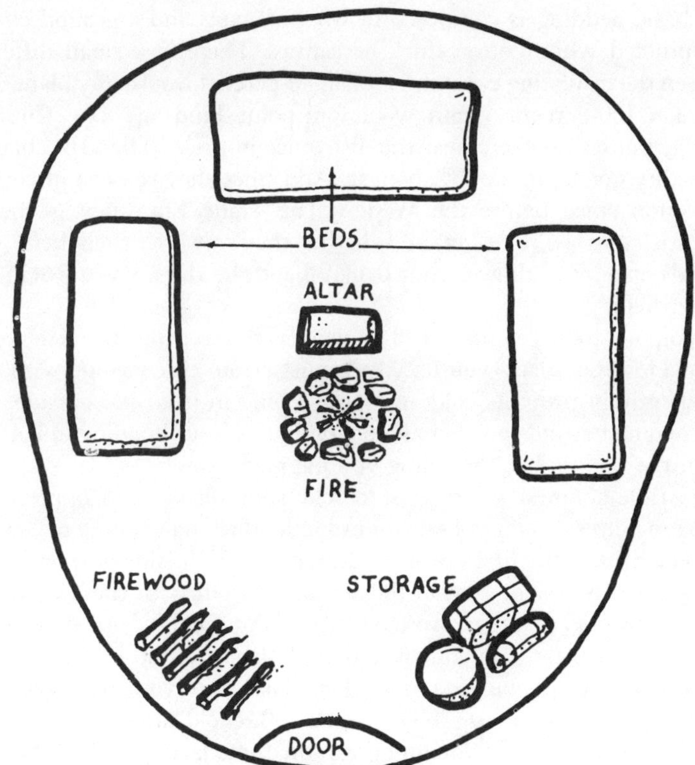

FIGURE 10–1   Typical tipi "floor plan." Indian lodges were generally erected with the door facing east.

a puff from a pipe or a swig from a jug, as it is being passed to the left. And you don't pass the pipe, jug, or whatever past the door. It goes, without being sampled, all the way back around to the right until it reaches the person nearest the door on the south side, then makes the round leftward again. It's bad manners to refuse eats, drinks, or smokes in a lodge.

Not everyone follows these practices, but you should be aware of them.

You may find that the owner of the lodge you're visiting has established a small altar just west of the firepit. It may be little more than a small square of scraped ground. It symbolizes Mother Earth and sometimes offerings of incense are burned there, or the ashes of the medicine pipe scraped out there. The lodge owner may be putting on the dog, or he may be serious about it. In any case, don't make fun.

A Buckskinner's Bedroll

Your basic bedding is composed of wool blankets and a ground cloth of waterproofed white cotton duck or canvas. There is a small difference between the insulating capabilities of an 80-percent wool army blanket and that of a 100-percent virgin wool four-point Hudson's Bay Company blanket, but it's nowhere near the difference in price. The HBC blankets are quality goods, no doubt about it. And since they've been in constant production since before the Western Fur Trade Era, they go beyond authenticity—they're originals. Whether they're worth their hefty price depends on a lot of things, your bankroll and the climate you live in chief among them.

In cold weather, you may need as many as three or four blankets to keep warm. However many you use, you must create an envelope with them that effectively prevents cold air from seeping in from the outside. This means going beyond the obvious step of folding your bedding in half with you in the middle like the filling of a big taco.

The time-honored solution is to fold your blankets in opposite and alternating directions. Let's say, for example, that you're going to use three blankets: Spread the first one out full, with the right side of it over where you plan to lay down. Spread the second one out with the *left* side over your bed area, so that they overlap halfway. Put the third one down smack on top of the first. Lay down and fold the top, middle, and bottom blankets over you, one after the other. That puts you in the center of something more like an egg roll than a taco. But cold air can still come in at your feet. Reach behind you and grasp the three layers of blankets you're lying on. Bite the layers on your chest. You can now sit up without them peeling off you. With your free hand, tuck the bottom end of the blankets beneath your feet. You are now snugly embedded—as long as you don't move.

If you do toss around in your sleep, or if you're a big man or just tall, frankly the above system doesn't work worth a damn. I believe wool blankets must have some sort of magnetic properties that cause one to repel another as the same poles of two magnets do.

What I do when the weather is nasty is take some knitting yarn and a big needle and stitch my blankets up across the bottom and halfway up the side. In really cold weather, I'll stitch them separately, then stuff one inside the other, alternating the half-open sides in the same spirit as the method described above. What I wind up with is an effective, yet primitive, sleeping bag. Be it known, however, that you not only have to ease into such a narrow bag, but you have to *ease* out of it, too. You don't want to sleep in anything like this around horses. And you might find yourself severely testing your bladder just to avoid the toil of getting out of bed.

On cold nights a buckskinner's bedroll is incomplete without a wool stocking (or voyageur's, or liberty) cap. You must keep your head warm.

Another essential, whether you're going to be a guest in a lodge or not, is a ground cloth. Waterproofed white canvas, a few feet longer and wider than your pallet, is standard equipment. It serves as a waterproof covering for your bedroll when you're knocking about, and will one day become part of the flooring for your own tent.

Canvas can be waterproofed with commercial preparations which are brushed or sprayed on. Hardware stores sell it. You can also brush on linseed oil, allowing ample time for each coat to dry before applying another.

Tents

Now you're at the point of buying your own shelter, becoming a lodge owner in the community of buckskinners. Please. Don't think it *must* be a tipi.

The tall, beautiful Indian lodges have a couple of strikes against them before the game begins. They may have been the epitome of portability in the days of the unfenced plains, when The People had dogs and horses to lug things around and plenty of time to kill. Nowadays those long poles present a heck of a logistics problem. Granted, it can be solved, and a lot of 'skinners do it with special racks or trailers. But for a two- or three-day campout, the hassle of packing and erecting a tipi is hardly worth it.

In spite of that, tipis are still the most popular rendezvous shelter. Partly it's a reflection of the overemphasis bucksinners tend to place on the Indian culture, and partly it's a self-perpetuating myth—the product of 'skinners learning their history from other 'skinners. You, a newcomer, go to a rendezvous and see a bunch of tipis and you just naturally assume the tipi was the mountain man's favorite tent.

In "Some Notes On Tents in the Western Fur Trade" (*The Museum of the Fur Trade Quarterly*, Spring, 1980), editor Charles Hanson says most fur trade tents were of the wedge style. The wedge tent common to the trade caravans and big company operations was a wall tent without walls, if you will. Think of a large, steep-sided pup tent. Hanson also cites the frequent use of make-shift lean-tos and "sleeping bowers" of semi-wickiup construction.

Mountain men sometimes wintered in Indian lodges, and those who married into the tribes might live in one year-round. But most mountaineers—be they traders, company men, or free trappers—stuck with something more portable.

(The white cotton canvas most buckskinning shelters are made of isn't strictly authentic, according to Hanson. Canvas during the fur trade era was a coarse linen. And tipis were made of skins, not canvas as they are today. But as long as you stay primitive in form and within the bounds set by your fellow 'skinners, cotton canvas is fine.)

So what type of shelter is for you? It may be nothing more than a ten-by-ten tarp. With a handful of rifle balls and a fifty-foot length of quarter-inch sisal or Manila hemp-rope, you can transform a tarp into a lean-to or diamond shelter.

Secure the guy lines to the tarp, by placing a rifle ball on the inside wherever you want a tie. Then mold the canvas around the ball and bind it

Two lean-tos, face-to-face, may not be as magnificent as the tipis in the background, but they are much easier to pack around, set up, and take down.

securely with an unraveled hank of the rope (Figure 10-2). Use a long enough piece to form a loop for guys or stakes.

When draped over a pole suspended between two forked sticks, staked at one end, and guyed at the other, your tarp becomes a lean-to (Figure 10-2). Or guy one corner off a tree trunk, stake down the other three, and put a tie in the middle so you can hoist it up by means of an overhanging branch, and you have a diamond shelter (Figure 10-3). Or you can simply roll yourself and your bedding up in the tarp to keep the dew off on a clear night or when you have to make a hasty camp.

Lean-tos with sides, from the one-man size to the big Bakers and Whelens, are available commercially. For appearances' sake, stay away from dyed canvas, particularly olive drab, and disguise metal grommets by stitching around them with artificial sinew.

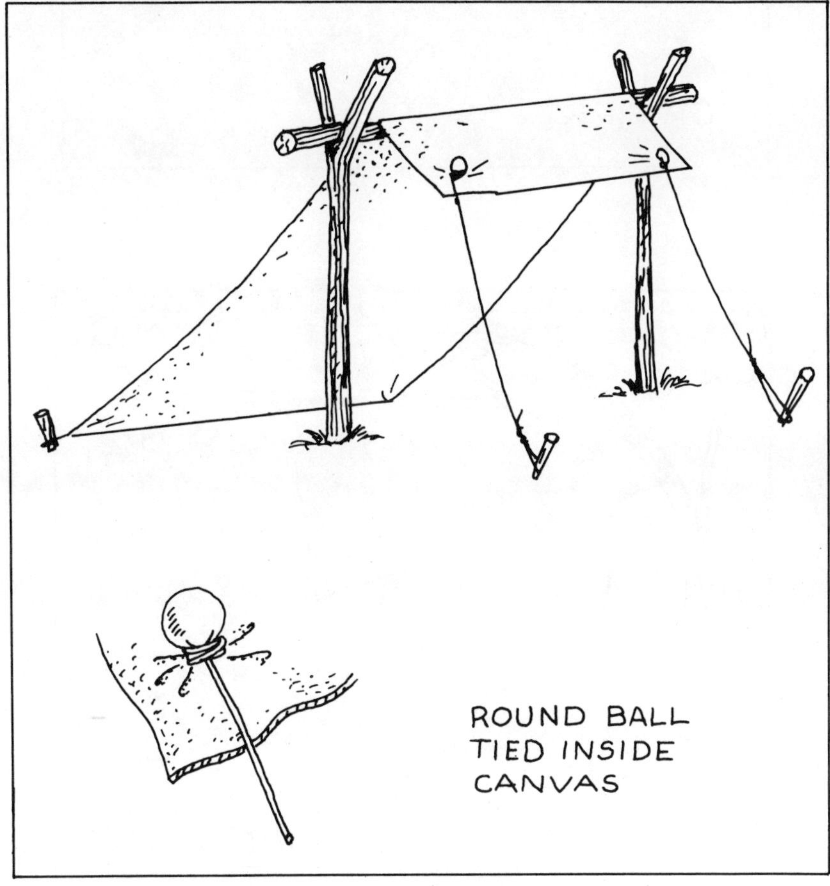

FIGURE 10–2 Basic lean-to rigged with a square tarp showing how to secure guy lines to the tarp.

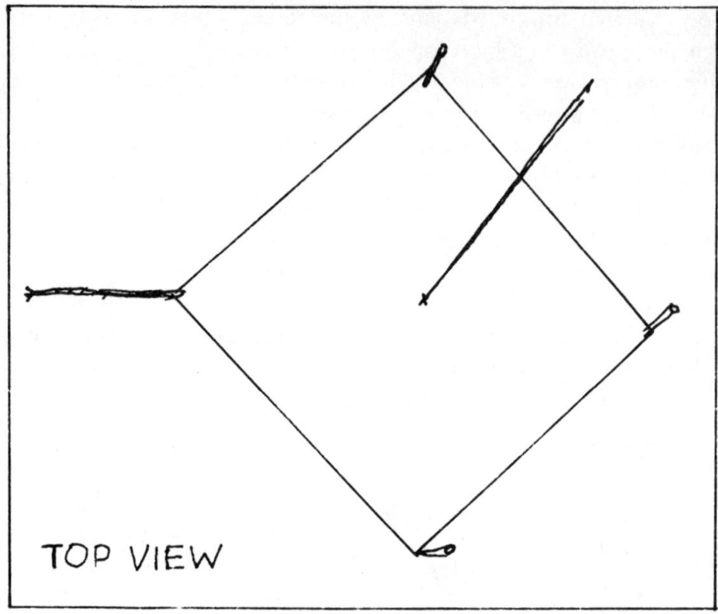

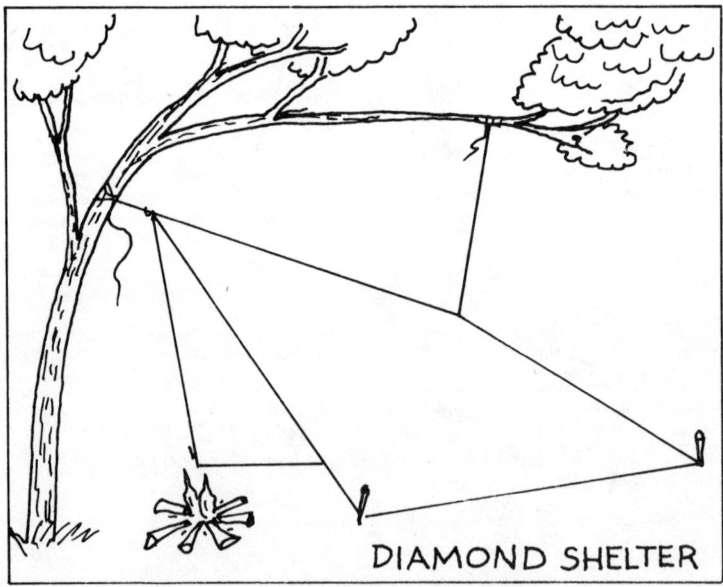

Figure 10–3   Diamond shelter rigged with a square tarp.

The awning of this lean-to can be let down. It also has side flaps, folded on top of the awning in this photo, which will seal the lean-to from all but the worst of weather. (Photo by Gene Hyre)

My favorite "primitive" shelter is a thoroughly modern hybrid of the lean-to and tipi. There are probably several manufacturers of these tents now, but one of the earliest and most prolific is Terrapin Ridge Lean-to & Tepee Co., which calls its product the Leanpee. You can put it up with five poles, three braced up by a bipod, or hang it from a tree branch and stake it down. It's dry, roomy, and can be heated pretty well with a candle lantern. I doubt any mountain man ever saw one, but it's definitely primitive in form and function.

The rendezvousing couple or family may want to consider the wall tent. It's roomy and, most important, relatively easy to pitch and transport. In moderately cold weather, you can keep it cozy with a few candle lanterns (the use of which should always be with due caution, you understand). For colder weather, some folks use those lightweight wood stoves popular in mountain hunting camps, the kind where you run the stovepipe through an asbestos patch in the tent roof. A wall tent isn't terribly authentic for a Rocky Mountain rendezvous, particularly with a portable wood stove inside, but they are accepted.

This Leanpee, a combination of tipi and lean-to designs, kept the author dry and warm on an outing in Adirondack Mountains when the temperature fell to twenty-eight degrees, with sleet. Heat was generated by a small fire set against the rock reflector in front of the tent.

Tipi Living

In spite of all the bad things I've said about tipis (indeed, in spite of all the bad things there *are* about tipis) I, too, am in love with that ancient shelter, the majestic palace of the prairie. I consider it the finest tent ever crafted, and if you can adapt it to these cursed modern times of apartment living and compact cars and hurried schedules, then it will serve you well.

The two most important facts about a tipi are that it is a tent within a tent, thereby providing an insulating layer of air between you and the elements, and that it has a built-in ventilation system that allows you to maintain a fire inside for convenience and warmth.

A tipi has a liner, a canvas curtain really, that hangs inside the poles all around from about chest height. It's long enough so that a foot or so overlaps the ground. With this overlap tucked inward and floor coverings such a tarps, carpet, or skins placed over it, you find yourself in a weatherproof "cup" within the tipi.

Heat from the fire inside the lodge causes the air inside to rise, drawing more air from beneath the tipi cover. This rising column of air pulls smoke upward and out through the smoke hole, which is why you're able to have a fire inside and not be smoked out. Flaps on either side of the smoke hole shelter it from rain and direct the flow of the air around the hole so that the smoke is carried away. In a deluge with no wind, it would probably be necessary to extinguish the fire and overlap the flaps, closing the smoke hole. With just about any rainfall some water will run down the lodge poles. If the poles are smooth and the liner is hung correctly, though, the water will run harmlessly between the liner and the cover.

Tipis are sized by the diameter of their "floor plans." Comercially-made tipis typically come in sizes of sixteen, eighteen, twenty, and twenty-two feet. A sixteen-footer, will accommodate mama, papa, and a couple of kids nicely over a long weekend. If you're going to camp for more extended periods, or entertain a lot, you would be better off starting with one of the mid-sizes. The twenty-two-footer is really spacious. David "Cripple Creek" Higginbotham has one affectionately dubbed the Higginbotham Hilton in which he once fed rattlesnake to twenty-seven 'skinners at one sitting with room, but not snake meat, for more.

The old mountain men were probably familiar with the four-pole lodge (using a foundation of four poles instead of a tripod), since all their major allies except the Snakes and sometimes the Nez Perce used them. Most commercial tipis today are of the simpler, stronger three-pole design, usually Cheyenne or Sious in origin.

Anyone even vaguely interested in Indian lodges owes it to himself to pick up a copy of *The Indian Tipi: Its History, Construction and Use*, by Reginald and Gladys Laubin. It's a classic.

Strike a Light

Firestarting in a primitive camp is, or should be, done in a primitive manner. That could mean sawing away with a firestarting bow, or chanting to Wako'da to send lightning, but usually it means breaking out flint and steel. It does not mean using wooden matches in place of flicking your Bic. Matches of sorts were around during the Western Fur Trade Era, but they were impractical for western travel.

A good firestarting kit consists of:

A striker or firesteel. This is a piece of extra-hard steel, typically C-shaped so that it fits over your fingers like brass knuckles.

Flint or chert. You'll need a sharp-edged chunk of flint or chert big enough to hold securely between your thumb and index finger. A musket flint will do.

While not strictly authentic for the period, the wall tent is excellent for some rendezvousing couples and families because it's easier than a tipi to erect, transport, and store. This "lodge" with its table, chuck box, and sheepherder's stove, is more appropriate for the gold rush years than the mountain fur trade period.

Charcloath to catch the spark, made of thick 100-percent cotton cloth roasted in a closed container so that it blackens without combusting.

Tinder, which can be any material combustible enough to be ignited by the glowing piece of charcloth.

Your tinder and charcloth should be kept in a container sufficiently waterproof to withstand a good dunking should your canoe capsize or your horse throw you while crossing a creek. The buckskinning supply outfits have replicas of original tinderboxes, but any metal container will do if you can remove obvious traces of the twentieth century from it. I used a japanned musket-cap tin, a modern container made to look old-fashioned by blackening in a fire, then polishing the smoke-borne "varnish." An application of beeswax around the rim helps to waterproof it. You shouldn't carry your flint and firesteel in the tinderbox as the weight of these objects, shifting around as you walk, is likely to pulverize your delicate charcloth.

The best material I've found to make charcloth is faded old blue jeans.

Putting up a tipi, even a small 16-footer like this one, can be toilsome. Most skinner's use the three-pole foundation, starting with a tripod and laying the other poles in the crotches. Finally, the cover is lifted on by means of the last pole, as this youngster is laboriously doing. The cover is then pinned in front and pegged down around the bottom.

Remember, it must be 100-percent cotton; the synthetics will shrivel and melt when heated. The denim is thick enough to easily catch and hold a spark. Thin polished stuff like a bedsheet doesn't work nearly as well.

To make charcloth you need a can with a tight-fitting metal lid. I use one that Kodak bulk film came in, but I suppose the possibilities are endless. Poke a small hole, about like the one an ice pick would make, in the center of the lid. Pack pieces of the material loosely in the can, close it up and put it on the fire. You can use a bed of coals or the heating element of an electric range. After a while, smoke will start shooting out of the hole in the lid. As soon as it quits or abruptly tapers off, that's the time to snatch the can off the heat. If you let it go too long, your charcloth will crumble and be useless. Let the can cool before opening it. If a blast of oxygen hits the cloth while it's still hot, it may go up in flames right then and there.

Michael "Two Bears" Hughes, the quintessential buckskinner, carries his charring can afield. Sitting around the campfire after dinner, puffing on his pipe, he'll toss the can on the coals for a bit. The stuff that's ready he'll take out and put in his tinderbox, replacing it with fresh pieces, even if he has to sacrifice some pillow-ticking patching for his rifle. The can always contains charcloth in varying stages of readiness.

The first step in starting a fire with flint and steel is the same as it would be if you were using a match: You make a little tipi of squaw wood layered over with slightly larger sticks so that your burning tinder will have something to ignite. Have enough wood handy to feed the fire until it really catches.

Fashion a nest of your tinder. I use jute, the rope-like stuff they make macrame with, and I keep a coil of it in my tinderbox. I just cut off a couple inches and fuzz it up. If you have plenty of charcloth, put a small piece, about the size of your thumbprint, in the nest.

Now take another piece of charcloth, maybe a little larger, and hold it on top of your flint, both pinched between thumb and forefinger. Line a frayed edge of the cloth up with the sharp edge of the flint. With a downward, glancing blow, hit the sharp edge of the flint with the striker. As soon as a spark lands on the charcloth, blow on it gently. When the spark begins to glow and spread, put the charcloth in the nest and continue blowing, or wave it back and forth to fan the spark.

When the tinder ignites, it'll go up quickly, so be prepared to thrust it under your squaw wood without knocking the stack over. If you have done the first step correctly, you'll soon have a good, strong fire.

In wet weather you can help things along with resin-rich pine knots or chunks of candle. But there's no substitute for good charcloth and dry tinder.

Well, maybe one. Sprinkle a little FFFFg in the squaw wood and twigs, fill the pan of an *uncharged* flinter, and spark it with the lock down beside the firepit. Sometimes it works, sometimes it doesn't.

Good 'skinners even use flint and steel to light their cigars and pipes, replacing matches and lighters with a piece of glowing charcloth.

Cookware and Containers

Buckskinners are contantly coping with the problem of what to put things in. Here you are, crosslegged in a well-appointed lodge, munching on venison stew in tip cups, and your host whips out a saltshaker filched from Howard Johnson's. It's the little things that dampen the atmosphere of the rendezvous.

Small powder horns such as those used for priming powder make excellent containers for dry spices. I carry oil for my firearms in an ancient corked medicine bottle I picked up at a flea market for something like a

Like Michael "Two Bears" Hughes, a good 'skinner will light up with smoldering charcloth, not a Zippo or Bic.

quarter. The solutions are all around, if you'll just use your imagination. Leather pouches, canvas or soft cloth bags, wooden boxes, cans—many of these items are readily available today and can be pressed into the buckskinning service. You can also go the super-authentic route and make up your own painted rawhide parfleches. But by all means, make some attempt to use reasonably appropriate containers in place of flagrantly modern ones.

Take water for example. Many 'skinners still carry water to the rendezvous in modern plastic water jugs, covering them with canvas or hides. You might succeed in preserving the atmosphere with that method, but you're tainting the spirit of the primitive camp. The better solution would be to invest in a wooden cask coated on the inside with beeswax (many of the outfits listed in Chapter 7 carry them). That way you don't have to act like a sneak thief every time you dip into your water supply.

Replicas of nineteenth-century canteens are abundant, or you can make your own out of a gourd or an old bottle covered with wool or leather to protect it.

As for cookware, cast iron is best but it's heavy. A sheet-steel skillet is lighter and will do a lot for you. I usually get by with nothing more than two tin cups, a small one for drinking and the big two-pint "military" size for whomping up one-pot meals and boiling coffee.

The more elaborately furnished lodges—those which wind up feeding everyone in camp at one time or another—are usually equipped with a

An oak cask, lined with beeswax and fitted with a spigot, is a good way to supply your primitive camp with water. The tripod stand and handy cup make this supply as handy as the home tap.

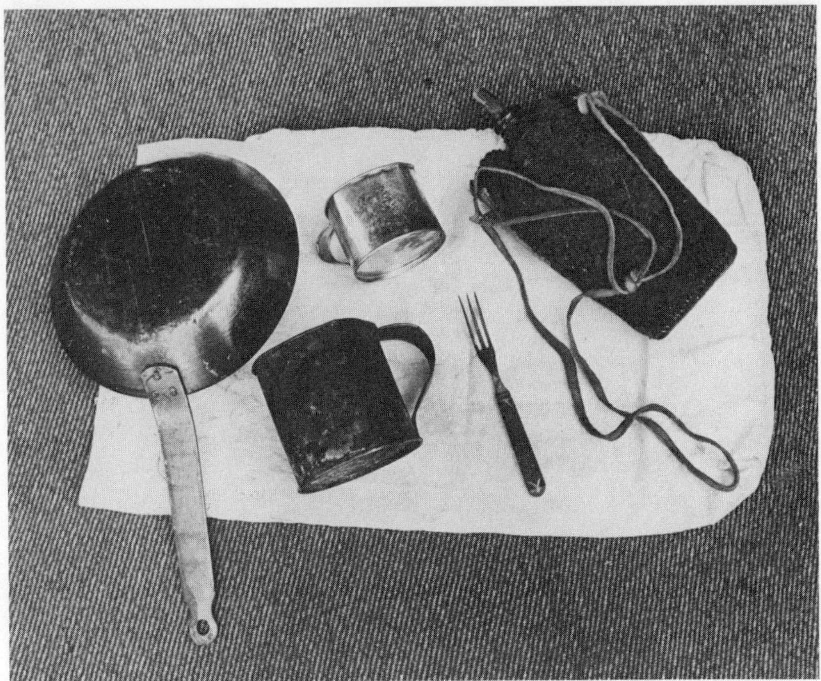

A buckskinner's basic mess kit. The canteen is an antique bottle flask covered in blanketing. Food is carried in the canvas ditty bag. The large tin cup shows evidence of use as a stew/coffee pot.

chuck box that serves as a pantry, storage for cookware and utensils, cutting board, and kitchen counter. These can be made to look primitive if you stay away from plywood and use heavy leather straps (or at least handwrought hinges) in place of metal hinges.

Fire Irons, Lanterns, and More

If you're going to drive into your primitive camp, go by canoe, or lead a pack animal, then a set of fire irons is well worth its weight and bulk. The common set would have two uprights which are pounded into the ground at opposite ends of the fire. At their tops they have forks or rings to hold the horizontal spit. There are also S-shaped hooks for suspending pots with bails from the spit. And one upright is usually fitted with a ring-shaped grill, eight to twelve inches in diameter, that swings on an arm out over the fire and can be used to support pots without bails over the heat.

This typical set of fire irons includes a horizontal spit over the fire; uprights for supporting the spit; S-shaped hooks of different lengths for hanging pots; and a ring-shaped grill mounted on a swivel-arm for holding pots without bails or providing extra support for heavy pots.

Such an attachment is also great, when set a little off the fire, for keeping coffee or food warm.

Fire irons are generally wrought iron and sometimes gussied up with curlicues, rams' heads, and whatnot. Rendezvous is the best place to pick up a set of fire irons, and you'll probably find primitive-style spatulas, ladles, and long-handled forks on sale there, too.

Many primitive events permit the use of ice chests as long as they are kept out of sight or disguised. My choice would be to do without, but I'm in the minority.

There isn't any way you can disguise a gasoline lantern, so leave it home when you go to rendezvous. Once you've grown accustomed to the charm of a candle lantern, or a string of them, you'll probably find yourself using them even on modern campouts. They illuminate without obliterating the natural velvety softness of the night. And they're doggone cheap to fuel. Their principal drawback is that they are somewhat fragile, which can also be said of gasoline lanterns. If you shop around the various buckskinning supply catalogs, you can find collapsible candle lanterns which are ideal for toting around in pack baskets or saddlebags.

One item that will add immeasurably to your comfort in the primitive camp is an Indian backrest or lazy-back, the distinctive willow-rod mat that serves as a chaise lounge. An Indian backrest is simple to make, it just requires a little time. You can gather green willow shoots or use dowels. Line them up side by side so they form a trapezoid about five feet long, three feet wide at the "seat," and two feet wide at the top. If you're using willow, alternate butt end with tip. Dowels are relatively constant in thickness, so with them there is no difference between butt and tip. The sticks, whatever they are, should be about the thickness of a pencil.

String the mat together with artificial sinew threaded through holes drilled in the sticks and knotted at top and bottom ends of the mat.

Suspend the mat from a tripod of light poles about five feet long. the back of the mat should rest against two of the poles, and about two feet of the wide end of the trapezoid should lie on the ground as the seat of the lazy-back.

Properly arranged, these primitive easy chairs are quite comfortable, a great improvement over sitting crosslegged.

A Primitive Bathroom?

Many mountain men, particularly those with Indian wives, tended to keep clean-shaven. They may have gotten a little scraggly on the trail or trap line, but the rendezvous, which was their big social event of the year, was a time to be spruced up.

You may hear tales of men shaving with ax heads or bowie knives, but the mountain men, like all men of the time, shaved with a straight razor. *The Mountain Man's Sketch Book* (Vol. 2), by James A. Hanson and Kathryn J. Wilson, contains a drawing of a paddle-shaped wooden case for carrying a razor. A leather strop is glued to the back of the case.

Mirrors pose no great authenticity problem since looking glasses were big trade items during the period. You would want to eschew plastic frames, of course.

While straight razors are still sold, it's tough to find someone to teach you how to use one. Barber colleges have even quit teaching the skill, and barber supply companies don't carry razor hones or even strops. This is the age of the injector.

The first step, and in some ways the hardest, is to find a good razor. One test you can perform is to run your thumbnail down the side of the edge. If you detect any flex, the razor has a "soft spot" and will never be worth a hoot. Expect to pay high dollar, maybe as high as thirty of them, for a good razor. If you can find one in good shape, you might be better off with

A pair of lazy-backs, the Indian chaise lounge. This primitive "chair," actually a mat of springy willow rods or dowels, is a lot more comfortable than it might look. The mat is suspended by a tripod of sticks each about five feet long.

an old razor, made when quality counted for more than it does today.

The second step is to get your razor sharp. At some point, this is going to require a hone. And good razor hones are tougher to find than good razors. In the old days they used "Belgian hickory," which was petrified peat. An old-timer in the barber supply business told me that the last batch he ordered, some years ago, was drastically inferior—so he assumes the petrified peat mining industry has gone the way of the dinosaur.

The only way is to poll barber supply houses and barber shops until you find a bona fide razor hone they'll let you use. Don't use a standard whetstone or, heaven forbid, a ceramic sharpening stick. You'll probably ruin your razor.

You hone a razor by laying it nearly flat on the honing surface and drawing it away from the cutting edge. You strop a razor the same way. If your razor is a good one and you use the strop often, you may get by without a hone. Good strops are made of horsehide and they have a second strap of coarse linen for putting a fine finishing touch on the edge.

Really, the only way to learn to shave with a straight razor is to lather up and start shaving. But here are some basics:

• Hold the razor at about a fifteen-degree angle to your face. Work downward, with the growth of the whiskers, and in short, straight strokes. Avoid any slicing motion as a nasty cut might be the result.

• Keep your skin taut. This is usually accomplished by applying upward pressure to the skin of your face with the thumb of your free hand. Your thumb must stay dry for this work, and the usual method is to drape a towel over your shoulder and constantly wipe your thumb on it. (To be honest, I haven't researched the history of terry cloth, so I don't know if there were towels as we know them in the mountains during the fur trade period. I don't imagine the dog soldiers would get excited about you standing around in the early morning light with a towel on your shoulder, unless it said Holiday Inn or something like that on it. If you want to be certain it's authentic, use a piece of flannel.)

• To remove the remaining patches of sandpaper, go back over them *carefully*, this time moving the razor against the growth of the whiskers.

• Strop often.

• And be *careful!* When a straight razor says *gotcha!* it says it in a deep, booming voice.

Now I realize I have sort of backed into this subject of the primitive bathroom. Very few men will insist on shaving at all on a primitive outing, let alone with a straight razor. On the other hand, nearly everyone would like to brush their teeth and scrub up a little. And as ol' Buffler Moon can tell you, when you gotta go, you gotta go. The reason I approached it this way is that, frankly, there isn't much to say about how 'skinners brush their teeth, scrub their faces, and urinate and defecate. For the most part, they do it all pretty much like they do it at home.

Oh, I've seen 'skinners using twigs for toothbrushes and packing around original recipe pine-tar soap, but the vast majority don't carry it that far. What did the mountain men use for toilet paper? *I* don't know. For some reason, they didn't write an awful lot about going to the bathroom in their letters and journals. It really doesn't matter. Most rendezvous have "porta-potties" stationed all around with nice fluffy rolls of modern toilet paper inside. Even the hard-core American Mountain Men will allow TP on their super-primitive outings.

There are, it seems, *some* ties binding us to this century that no one really wants to break.

11

Trail and Camp Chow

We had just finished a truly scrumptious stew containing a droplet of meat from a dove Badger had collected with his trade gun and a scrawny squirrel ambushed by Black Kettle. But it consisted mostly of trail foods I had prepared in advance—venison jerky, and dehydrated potatoes and carrots. Yes, and some "wild onions" picked and so labeled by Cripple Creek.

I got the blame for the whole thing, but I want to reiterate: Creek. Picked. The Onions.

He ate most of the stew, too, which was justice. He stood and announced in his typically casual manner, "Well, that was a mighty fine meal and I think I'll go puke."

And he did. Just that quick.

Buffler Moon and SFB were right behind him.

"Heeey, what's going on here?" someone wondered aloud.

"I don't *feel* sick. . . ." said Two Bears. The way he let it hang meant he wasn't ready to claim robust health, either. Not just yet.

"Neither me," said I.

"I feel fine," said Badger. He belched deeply.

"But I think we all should make ourselves throw up, just to get rid of whatever's bothering those guys," Two Bears said, sensibly.

So I headed into the darkness, prepared to stick a finger down my throat or something. But all I had to do was gag a couple of times and up it came.

"You sick, too?" came a voice over by the horses. It was Black Kettle.

"Naw, I'm just throwing up to get rid of whatever made the others sick. You better do it, too."

"OK. *Blaah!*" Just that quick.

In less than forty-five minutes, we had all upchucked except Badger. He did some heavy-duty belching. And no wonder. It turned out that Cripple Creek's "onions" were death camas, a poisonous member of the lily family.

The point of this tale—at least the one that's obvious to *me*—is that it

The author was involved in a lengthy shoot-out with a covey of quail before bagging this one bird. Living off the land is challenging; living out of your pack or saddlebags—with jerky and pemmican as cheap insurance—is less risky. (Photo by Larry Bozka)

takes a better naturalist than I am to be out grazing like that. Also, while I'm only too happy to eat any fish I catch or animals I shoot, I've been skunked enough to know that you can't count on catching fish or shooting animals. If you're going to eat while you're on the move in a primitive situation, you had better bring it with you.

Filling As Mud and Twice As Tasty

The kind of stuff you need on a canoe trip, trail ride, or walk-in, or in a no-frills primitive hunting camp, is food that delivers energy yet is lightweight and compact, doesn't need to be kept on ice, and is easy to prepare. It would be nice if it tasted good, too, but you can't have everything.

For the purpose of making trail foods, I strongly recommend you invest in a dehydrator. It tremendously broadens the range of food items you can carry in your pack basket or saddlebags. Even if you do mostly modern camping, the freshness—and low cost—of home-dehydrated foods will make you throw rocks at the freeze-dried stuff. The investment in a dehydrator need not be large, because it's easy to make one with inexpensive materials. More about that later.

Other "authentic" foods like oatmeal, cornmeal, salt pork, and flour are ready to go right out of the grocery store.

The Big Three in the mountain man's traveling pantry are jerky, pemmican, and hardtack. Of these, pemmican offers the most complete range of food values. Jerky is the tastiest. 'Tack is ... well, it *is* filling.

A simple homemade dehydrator has four 100-watt bulbs for heat and a small electric blower to circulate moist air out of the box. The trays are window screens made to fit the box.

Few of us today live in circumstances that allow us to make jerky the old-time way, by stringing raw meat out and letting it dry in the sun. The neighbors wouldn't appreciate it, although their dogs certainly would. You can dry meat in a regular oven, but this takes a long time and heats up the house; anyway, the jerky usually turns out too dry and brittle to be reconstituted in a stew, one of jerky's better uses.

Jerky made in a dehydrator becomes juicy and tender when boiled in a pot of water for a while. If you throw in dehydrated vegetables like potatoes, carrots, and onions, along with seasoning and a pinch of flour, you wind up with an excellent beef (venison, elk, whatever) stew.

Since fat will not dry properly, jerky must be made with lean meat—ultimately its greatest shortcoming. I have found, however, that marinating meat in a light vegetable oil doesn't retard the drying process appreciably yet helps to seal in flavor. It also seems to help seasonings like salt, pepper, and garlic powder permeate the meat.

Since I dry my jerky on screen trays rather than on racks of green sticks, I don't bother with paring chunks of meat out into long strips the way the Indians and frontiersmen did. I would just have to cut it up to put it in a stew, anyway. Nor do I worry much about the grain. I merely strive to keep each piece no thicker than a quarter of an inch. After the jerky is done, I separate the pieces that happen to be cut across the grain and put them where they can be easily reached for snacking on dry. The other pieces go for stew meat.

As a dry trail food, eaten right out of the bag, jerky leaves a lot to be desired. Without fat, your body can't make the most of the proteins in the lean meat. That's where pemmican comes in.

The original Indian trail food, pemmican is definitely not the kind of stuff you sit around munching on while watching a game on TV. It's greasy, and even the best of it can be a touch nasty tasting. But when outdoors exerting yourself, especially in cold weather, you will positively crave the grease. For all its nastiness, pemmican is an efficient fuel for an overworked body.

It's made of pulverized jerky, suet, and, more often than not, dried fruit. Squaws used to pound jerky in stone or wooden mortars, or simply crush it between two rocks. I use a common kitchen blender. Set on "chop" or "grate"—the medium speed range—the blender turns adequately dried jerky into a coarse, grayish-tan powder. Put this powder into the sort of pan you would use to make brownies—an inch and a half or two inches thick.

I strongly recommend you add some sort of fruit at this point to give your pemmican better flavor. Raisins are good because they add a lot of food value. Or run some blueberries through your dehydrator. With a dehydrator, your imagination is the limit. Mix the fruit and the powdered meat as uniformly as you can.

Jerky made in a dehydrator can be given a smoked flavor by placing the dehydrator into a "smokehouse" made by sealing off a tent and building a smoky fire in it. Here the author adds sodden hickory chips to the fire.

Finally, pour in just enough melted beef suet to cake the ingedients together. (Suet is obtained by heating fat in an iron skillet or pot over a low heat until the liquid is rendered. The rendered liquid dries to form a cream-colored paste which keeps quite well without refrigeration. Your friendly neighborhood butcher will sell you fat trimmings, probably cheap.)

After thoroughly mixing all the ingredients, cut the pemmican cake into cubes, or mold it into balls, and store it in a tightly stitched cloth or leather bag. A bait of pemmican will got practically untouched at rendezvous. But believe me, on a walk-in, canoe trip, or trail ride, you'll be turning the bag inside out and longing for more.

You won't think much of hardtack with your first taste of it, either. But you'll be glad you brought it along on any outing where your time around the campfire is limited.

'Tack is made by mixing two cups of flour, a half-tablespoon each of salt and sugar, and half a cup of water. Roll the dough out until it's about a quarter of an inch thick, cut it into square biscuits or crackers (whichever term appeals to you), and bake it at 350 degrees Fahrenheit for thirty minutes.

If you put a couple of chunks of 'tack in a cup along with some dried fruit, soak it overnight, and heat it alongside the morning coffee, you'll have a passable cobbler with which to greet the new day.

Dehydrated Vegetables

Just about any fresh vegetable can be dried and later reconstituted in water, sometimes with startling results. Clusters of cauliflower, for example, shrink down to shapeless gray flakes the size of a fingernail, then pop back to original size in boiling water. If you cook them in a stew long enough, dehydrated potatoes, onions, and carrots become indistinguishable from fresh ones.

I have found that chunks or slices of potato will turn an unappetizing soot color in the dehydrator. But the problem is solved by first soaking them for an hour in a solution of one tablespoon of salt and juice of half a lemon to two quarts of water.

Dried vegetables like cauliflower or carrots may not be strictly authentic for the mountain man's diet, but you can pack them around the way the mountain man carried his food and they certainly add variety to your trail menu.

The same may be said for salt pork. "Pork-eater," in case you didn't know, was an especially uncomplimentary synonym for pilgrim or newcomer. (Nowadays, it's a friendly synonym, so don't get your back up if somebody hails you with it.) Supposedly the term arose because newcomers to the mountain fur trade would gobble up great amounts of the company's salt pork instead of their own fresh-killed meat. But let me tell you what, you spend eight hours paddling a canoe down an icy stream, then beach near a fire where someone is frying up a bait of salt pork, and you'll become a willing and ravenous "pork-eater" yourself, as soon as you can get near enough to stab a fork in the pan, no matter *how* long you've been a 'skinner.

Along with the pork, be sure to bring along a sackful of cornmeal. Mixed with water and a pinch of salt to about the consistency of pancake batter, simple cornmeal becomes the fixin's for Johnny cakes. And mighty satisfying they are, too, especially if you have time to reconstitute some dehydrated onions to mix in the batter. Just fry them in the grease until they brown lightly and they're ready.

Rendezvous Cooking

Chow at the rendezvous is pretty much like any camp cooking. You'll see sweet breads being prepared in Dutch ovens or open skillets, lots of stews and chilis, and occasionally someone will roast up a beaver just for show.

In the typical rendezvous, you can drive right up to your campsite, so your only limitation in the amount of food you can carry is the available cargo space in the family vehicle. Many—make that most—rendezvous allow ice chests as long as they are covered up.

Even with the loose authenticity rules, though, there has to be some common sense applied or the whole atmosphere of the rendezvous will come crashing down on our costumed heads. Don't turn your kids out to wander around camp with popsicles in hand. Pour canned and bottled

Dutch ovens and other cast-iron cookware are popular with 'skinners who drive to and from rendezvous and aren't concerned about weight.

beverages into appropriate containers—gourds, tin cups, etc.—and immediately stash the cans and bottles out of sight. Don't let bottle caps and snap-tabs (called "beer claws" at primitive gatherings) get away from you. And if you can force yourself to do it, leave those paper towels at home. I know they're the next best thing to mosquito dope for camping, but they are unsightly in a primitive setting.

As for the old-timers, there's no question that they ate jerky and pemmican, and even salt pork when the need arose. But the day you lower a young buck to the ground with your muzzleloader and sit around the fire that same evening dining on fresh deer liver sprinkled with chopped onions and sauteed in bacon grease, then you'll really be capturing the spirit of mountain man eatin'.

The fur trappers were, perforce, meat eaters. By most accounts, they favored buffalo, and loved nothing so much as a hump rib roasted over an open fire. But they could go a long way on boiled beaver tail, too. During the long days on the trap line in spring and fall, mountain men ate a lot of beaver and other small game taken incidentally.

Like the Indians, the mountaineers consumed their animals guts and all. It's the only way a man can survive on a pure meat diet. One of their favorite delicacies was what the French-Canadians among them called *boudin*, great lengths of buffalo intestine stuffed with minced liver, kidney, and other "by-products." Somewhere in the literature is described a scene in which two mountaineers are sitting crosslegged on opposite sides of a dirty saddle blanket, upon which is a huge coil of greasy *boudin*. Each man is wolfing down an end of the coil and counting himself dead and gone to heaven.

The Cajuns of Louisiana still make *boudin* (pronounced boo-dan, as only a Frenchman can say "dan"), although mostly of pork parts. There's what they call red *boudin*, which is a blood sausage and getting harder to find, and white *boudin*, in which the pork parts are made into a kind of rice dressing. The taste for white *boudin*, like crawfish, has become something of a Louisiana export, and you might be able to find some in your neck of the woods. It would make a nice "replica" of the buffalo *boudin* of bygone times.

Many rural Cajuns, even today, use a short length of cow horn as a funnel for stuffing *boudin*, something to bear in mind in the event you get the urge to stuff some yourself.

At this point, I'd like to put in a purely personal plug for what I like to call the buckskinner's vitamin. Garlic. Raw garlic. Col. Mike Powasnick, who spends a lot of time in Italy in consort with the manufacturers of his Trail Guns Armory line, brought a mess of it on a trip several of us took to the Great White North. He gobbled a whole clove every morning with coffee. The rest of us took to eating it, too, in self-defense. Now, if you listen to folklore, garlic will prevent anything from gout to vampire-bite.

A roasting beaver gives this rendezvous setting an extra touch of authenticity. Most rendezvous meals, though, are more on the order of stew, gumbo, and chili.

"The Rabbit Hunt," by Frederic Remington. During long days on the trap line in spring and fall, mountain men often had to rely on small game for food. (Courtesy of The Thomas Gilcrease Institute of American History and Art, Tulsa, Oklahoma)

All I know is that the weather on that trip was *awful*, and we were unprepared for it, and yet not one of us came down with as much as a runny nose. I've been a believer ever since. Of course I have to use the garlic-oil pills the health-food stores sell when I'm at home. But afield I go "primitive" and eat raw garlic. It grows on you. I recommend it.

A Home-Built Dehydrator

To make my dehydrator, I started with a crude box made from some fiberboard I had lying around the garage. It turned out twenty-seven inches wide by thirteen inches high by eighteen deep. The dimensions are unimportant, I think. I've seen workable dehydrators in various sizes and shapes. (See Figure 11–1.)

The front is a door that opens downward, like the typical oven door. Unlike an oven door, however, it fits loosely, so there are gaps around the edges. As shown in the photograph earlier in this chapter, the door is hinged at the bottom, and the back of the box is full of holes. (I happened to have a piece of the kind of fiberboard that metal hooks fit into, which I could use for the back. Otherwise, I would have had to take out my

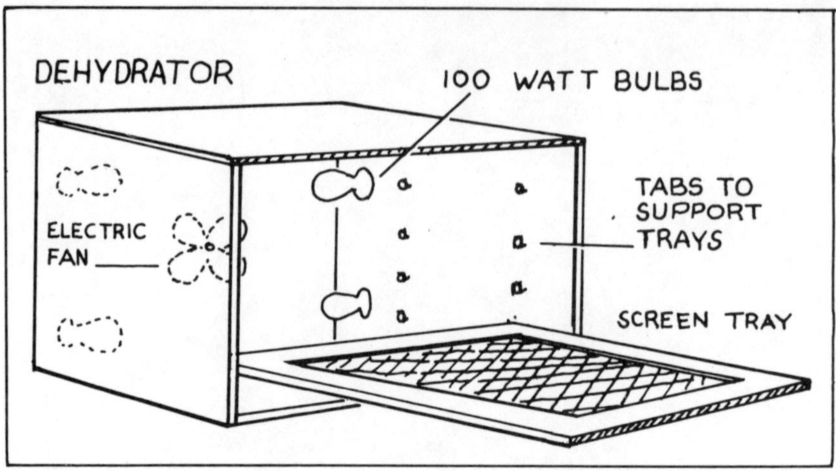

FIGURE 11–1   Design of a typical homemade dehydrator. The front door (not shown) opens downward and fits loosely so that air can enter.

electric drill.) So what I had at this point was a box through which air could flow, front to back and vice versa.

I installed four porcelain sockets toward the back, two on each side. They're for the 100-watt bulbs that are the heat source. (See Figure 11–2 for wiring schematic.)

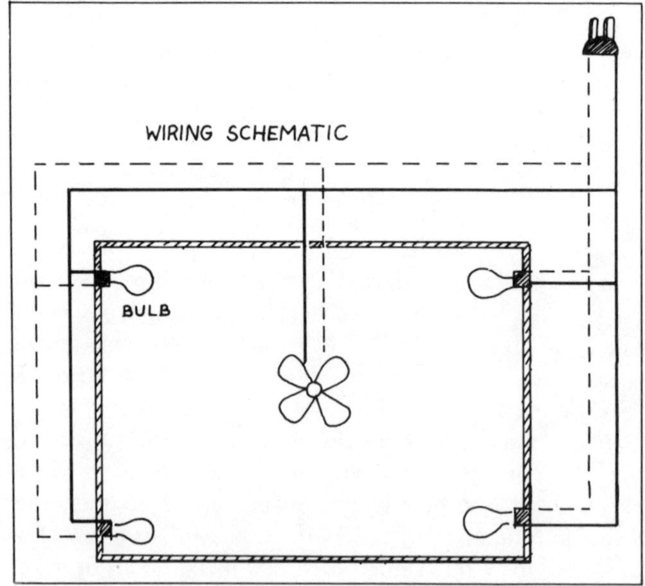

FIGURE 11–2   Wiring schematic for a dehydrator.

I now had a box with heat and ventilation.

Then I put in a small (½50-horsepower) electric fan of the type used to cool electronic gear, which cost about five bucks. Any small fan will do as long as it moves air in or out of the perforated back of the box.

I had a box with heat and *forced* ventilation.

And that's all in the world a dehydrator is. The air forced out of the box takes with it the moisture wrung out of the food by the light bulbs. Some of the store-bought dehydrators have thermostats in them, but I don't see any need for that. I simply dry the stuff until it'll rattle around in a Mason jar and pronounce it done.

For trays, I bought window-screen materials from the local home repair center and made screens to fit the box. They're held in place, stacked one atop the other about an inch apart, by little metal tabs used for mounting shelving. You could use nails, for that matter.

With a dehydrator, you can provision your primitive outings with a wide range of foods that require no cooling, take up little space, and weigh very little. And you won't need to pick "wild onions," or other unidentified goodies, to fill the pot.

12

Rendezvous!

You can't quite call it dawn, but there's a line of ghostly white cones where only moments before was a solid bank of charcoal-colored mist. Everything is still and silent. But you catch the faint smell of wood smoke, perfumed with the odor of boiling coffee. Folks are stirring somewhere near.

You kick up your own fire and soon you're relaxing with a steaming cup in hand, watching the tall lodges turn a pale shade of gold.

All at once there are more signs of life in camp: A kid of about ten manfully hauling a load of wood from the community pile, a younger sister tailing after him with one spindly branch, trying to tickle his ear; the smell and sound of bacon sizzling nearby; a woman's soft, melodious laughter somewhere on the far side of camp.

Early morning is one of the most beautiful things about a rendezvous—either the *most* beautiful or a close second, depending upon when you're trying to decide.

Living History

But a rendezvous is more than just a beautiful painting in motion, accompanied by equally charming sounds and smells. It's like a family reunion. Many of the people there will be among old friends they haven't seen in months, just as were the old-time trappers who came together in the summer after a long spring of trapping alone or in small groups. And just as with those mountain men, there is a camaraderie, a brotherhood, among buckskinners, be they old friends or strangers. To present yourself as a 'skinner at a rendezvous is to assert that you're the salt of the earth, and you're going to have to go a long way to prove differently.

A rendezvous is also a shoot, primitive and informal, but still a chance to test your skills against those of other muzzleloading enthusiasts.

As this painting by Alfred Jacob Miller reminds us, the mountain man was a mounted man, who never walked when he could ride. Many 'skinners today are trailering horses to primitive gatherings. (Courtesy of The Walters Art Gallery, Baltimore, Maryland)

And it's a huge buckskinner's flea market, where you can pick through such esoterica as antler buttons, quillwork, and firesteels—items you might otherwise have to order sight-unseen through the mail.

But mostly, a rendezvous is living history.

From the earliest years of European presence in North America, frontiersmen gathered to trade, visit, and engage in friendly shooting matches. But the Rocky Mountain rendezvous of the Western Fur Trade Era lasted only from 1825 to 1840. It was a political, economic, and social microcosm that changed the course of a nation, a tiny temporary oasis of civilization in a vast wilderness. It came to be a kind of rest stop for missionaries and settlers bound for Oregon. Indians throughout saw it as a combination fair and flea market wherein they might obtain the luxuries of the white man's world. It became, if not a true world's fair, at least a continental one, with Mexican citizens coming up from Taos with trade goods, Britons from the Pacific Northwest, Yankee entrepreneurs returning from California with strings of horses.

But the main purpose of the rendezvous was to exchange furs for supplies, the supplies staying in the mountains with the trappers and Indians and the furs going by return caravan to the market in St. Louis.

And when the demand for furs died, so did the rendezvous. (Some historians maintain there was no rendezvous in 1831. There was, but no trade caravan met it. This was the year, remember, when the Rocky Mountain Fur Company took over from Smith, Jackson, and Sublette, the three of whom had briefly entered the Santa Fe trade. Tom Fitzpatrick had to follow them to Santa Fe to purchase supplies, was late in returning to

Trade blankets turn the rendezvous into buckskinners' flea markets, and help preserve the atmosphere of the original gatherings which were essentially business conventions.

the mountains, and had to spend the fall tracking down the scattered trappers to distribute the supplies.)

A Rocky Mountain trapper in the 1830s made good money compared to the working stiffs back in the States. But mountain prices for trade goods—ammunition and blankets, traps and horses, tobacco and liquor, and the foofaraw to turn the ladies' heads—were outrageous. The mountain man spent more in a few weeks than his city cousin made in as many years.

And he had a grand time doing it, at least according to the account of mountain man Jim Beckwourth in his autobiography:

It may well be supposed that the arrival of such a vast amount of luxuries from the East did not pass off without a general celebration. Mirth, songs, dancing, shouting, trading, running, jumping, singing, racing, target-shooting, yarns, frolic, with all sorts of extravagances that white men or Indians could invent, were freely indulged in. The unpacking of the medicine water contributed not a little to the heightening of our festivities.

A jubilant free trapper comes rip-roaring into camp with dust in his throat and socializing on his mind. Nowadays, the rendezvous is more a retreat from the corrosive nature of civilization than from the hardships of the trap line.

In the movie *The Mountain Men*, there was a brief scene where, in the middle of a background of drunken confusion, a man inexplicably burst into flames. According to mountaineer Joe Meek, that really happened.

> It is reported by several of the mountainmen that on the occasion of one of these "frolics" one of their number seized a kettle of alcohol, and poured it over the head of a tall, lank, redheaded fellow, repeating as he did so the baptismal ceremony. No sooner had he concluded than another man with a lighted stick, touched him with the blaze, when in an instant he was enveloped in flames. Luckily some of the company had sense enough to perceive his danger, and began beating him with pack-saddles to put out the blaze. But between the burning and the beating, the unhappy wretch nearly lost his life....

Wild and crazy guys, those mountain men.

Modern rendezvous are parties, too, and if that's what you want, your cup will runneth over. But they're also family outings for many, and the revelers respect that. At today's rendezvous are some of the most considerate drunks in the world.

Maybe it's because a rendezvous is an armed camp, but I've never seen a fight or even a decent argument at one. Nor do you have to worry about wandering off and leaving your possessions in such a flimsy shelter as a tent. Traders leave entire stocks of goods, including expensive custom-made firearms, unattended on their trade blankets. I don't have any idea what the record is nationwide, but there's never been an incidence of theft at a function of the Texas Association of Buckskinners (TAB).

Buckskinning Organizations

Most rendezvous are arranged by one organization or another. Non-members are frequently welcome as newcomers, but you're expected to join up if you're going to make a habit of it.

The major organizations hosting the big rendezvous that draw participants from all over the country are the National Muzzle Loading Rifle Association (NMLRA), the National Association of Primitive Riflemen (NAPR), and The American Mountain Men (AMM). A "wildcat" rendezvous of sorts, albeit a big one, is sponsored annually by *Muzzleloader* magazine.

Then there are hundreds of smaller rendezvous held by regional groups such as the TAB, and there are even smaller "wildcats" in which someone with access to a site simply spreads the word of time and place.

The NMLRA is to the muzzleloading fraternity what the National Rifle

The symbols of the raucous old days are still around, like this skull atop a tipi door pole. But today's rendezvous are family gatherings, with activities for almost everybody, and are as tame or tamer than the average country fair.

Association is to shooters of modern-type firearms. It oversees formal target shooting, sponsoring the world series of black powder at its Friendship, Indiana, headquarters and many a lesser shoot. It cosponsors (with the NAPR) a big western rendezvous, holds another in the Midwest for the Old Northwest recreators, and yet another in the East for the modern longhunters. Plans were in the works for a fourth NMLRA rendezvous to accommodate our southwestern heritage.

For more information about its activities, or to find out about buckskinning groups in your area, write the National Muzzle Loading Rifle Association, Box 67, Friendship, Indiana 47021.

The NAPR was formed specifically to organize buckskinning on a national basis, and to hold the first big, pure rendezvous since 1840. Write the National Association of Primitive Riflemen, Box 885, Big Timber, Montana 59011.

The American Mountain Men started out as a survivalist group and, in awe of the survival skills of the old-time mountain men, turned toward historical recreation with the emphasis still on learning how to survive in the wilds. Membership in AMM is achieved and maintained only by fulfilling requirements in much the same way Boy Scouts earn merit badges. As you might expect, AMM rendezvous are among the most stringent when it comes to authenticity and are not really suitable for the

The social life at a rendezvous reminds us of the way neighborhoods were before that electronic fence-builder, television, came along.

rank beginner. To learn more about this elite group, write The American Mountain Men, Box 259, Lakeside, California 92040.

Cast of Characters

Rendezvous big and little are basically free-flowing occasions where everyone does his or her own thing. Most of them have certain events and a modicum of organizational structure in common, however.

The club official in charge of a rendezvous is called the booshway, which was the mountain man's way of saying *bourgeois*, a French term used in the old days as the title of the fur company employee in charge of the company's activities at an original rendezvous.

The booshway generally wears a crescent-shaped metal neckpiece called a *gorget*. The *gorget*, another French term, was the last vestige of nobleman's armor, worn symbolically to denote military authority by the time of the mountain fur trade. Indians loved them and they became popular chiefs' presents from the U.S. and British governments. It's doubtful a white bourgeois or partisan would have worn one as a badge of office, but buckskinning has evolved some customs all its own.

The "police force" at a rendezvous are the dog soldiers, patterned after the Indian camp police. Dog soldiers mostly enforce the dress code and authenticity rules for camp gear, match lost pets with their owners, and direct visitors to the john. They're usually identifiable by arm bands.

The dress code is probably the biggest headache, since it's based strictly on historical knowledge. Taste has nothing to do with it. The rendezvous is a time to show off, and that isn't a modern phenomenon. The old trappers donned their Indian-made finery and the Indians swathed themselves in the gaudiest trade cloth they could afford. The modern version gets to looking a little Halloweenish, but we have Joe Meek's word that the uniform of the day—in *his* day—consisted of "motley garb and brilliant coloring."

At a rendezvous, the term "pilgrim" generally applies to a newcomer in buckskinning, a person who has been accepted into the fold though he or she may still have a lot to learn. Casual visitors to a primitive camp are seldom granted the title. Apparently, the original mountain men first used the term to describe the missionaries who began showing up at rendezvous en route to the Oregon country. Later, any inexperienced traveler in the West was often called a pilgrim.

Hivernant is a French word that means "winter resident." In the old days it was used (originally by French-Canadians who staffed much of the fur trade operations in the Rocky Mountains as they had in the Old Northwest) to designate the men who lived year-round in the mountains. Today, a hivernant is a person acknowledged by his fellow buckskinners as

Texas Association of Buckskinners board member Keith Chambers wears the official TAB *gorget*. The last vestige of the nobleman's armor, the *gorget* was still being worn as a symbol of military rank during the Mountain Fur Trade Era. Many of today's mountain men use it as the booshway's (rendezvous leader's) badge of office.

excelling in nineteenth-century survival skills. An Hispanic version of the word, *hiverano*, is a high rank in The American Mountain Men, the most exacting organization in buckskinning.

Shoots and Other Contests

Where the accomplished 'skinner really shines, though, is in the various contests. As the sun climbs, the booshway or his representative elicits donations from the traders and craftsmen to be used as prizes in the competitions. You could say it's part of their overhead, like taxes, I suppose. But the items are given gladly—truly in the spirit of a donation.

The events are informal and there are usually separate-but-equal ones for women and children.

A typical shooting match is an elimination event. By turns, shooters step up to a stick on the ground, marking the firing line, and pot away offhandedly at, say, a skillet hanging in a tree. Miss and you're out. The firing line is moved back for the survivors and they go at it again, and again, until only one remains to take the prize.

The mountain man run is a little more elaborate, requiring a course with a series of targets that either pop up or come into view as the contestant advances. Time to complete the course and marksmanship are both accounted for in the scoring.

The stake shoot, a team event, is a test of firepower. The first team to shoot a wooden stake in two wins.

There are also pistol events like the Mike Fink shoot where you try to blast a tin cup off a pilgrim's head—in theory, of course, both cup and pilgrim being an artist's conception. If you can hit the cup drawn on the target instead of the pilgrim, the theory is it would have flown off his head.

There are tomahawk and knife throws, naturally, and firestarting contests with flint and steel, and even an occasional cook-off featuring ancient recipes.

Soon, it's time to head back to the lodge and rustle up some supper for yourself. Or dig out your spoon and cup and go visiting. Then, too, comes the "unpacking of the medicine water" and, for some, the absolute soaring of the festivities. Yarns are spun and the day's activities assume heroic proportions. Now and again some unabashed soul will rare back, like Brian Keith did so well in *The Mountain Men*, and give his my-Pappy-was-a-pistol-I'm-a-son-of-a-gun speech. If there are any musicians in camp (there always are), they'll find one another, to the audience's delight or chagrin.

Not quite as abruptly as the day began, but still suddenly enough to take you by surprise, the bustle of activity winds down. The rowdies have gone off to tip over an outhouse with an unfortunate—no doubt long, lank,

The rendezvous is increasingly a family affair. Once women found out how much fun it was, there was no way the patriarchs could keep it all to themselves. Probably the biggest beneficiaries are the kids—rendezvous are like living at Frontierland.

and redheaded—enthroned therein. You can still hear them, but it's like the yelping of coyotes in the far, far distance. More immediate conversations are in hushed tones. Once-blazing campfires now glow with that satisfying deep orange. Dozens of candle lanterns flicker in a random pattern, like Japanese lanterns over the patio when the party's over. It's a bit lonely—yet beautiful.

In fact it's the *most* beautiful scene the rendezvous has to offer. Or the second-most. It just depends on what time of day it is when you're trying to decide.

This 'skinner is aiming his round-butted plains pistol at the cup on Mike Finks' buddy's head. Note the stick that marks the firing line at his feet. As better replica and reproduction pistols come on the market, handgun events are becoming more frequent at primitive shoots.

Trap-setting contests are part of the fun at rendezvous. This modern long-spring trap is changed little from the traps used by the original mountain men. Many 'skinners run trap lines during open season on furbearers. (Photo by Gene Hyre)

13

Maximum 'Skinners

With its most sincere devotees, buckskinning has a way of going beyond a hobby and becoming a life-style. For a very few, it means actually staying year round in the mountains, and living off the land. Others make a business of buckskinning, by handcrafting guns or moccasins or tipis and traveling from rendezvous to rendezvous to sell and promote them. Most of us, though, have to find our own niche in the buckskinning scene within the fabric of everyday twentieth-century life. Each of us has our own way to carry buckskinning to the maximum.

Take Michael "Two Bears" Hughes, for example. If you spot him at a rendezvous, you instantly know he belongs there. He has a custom-made Hawken and a homemade Northwest trade gun. He wears a war shirt of deer skins he brain-tanned himself. He has a well-appointed lodge, a horse, and an Indian pad saddle. He's even married to an Indian lady. It's not enough.

"I love the rendezvous, you *know* that," he says. "Love to party and visit and generally make a fool of myself. But more and more, I've been wanting to experience what the other eleven months of the mountain man's life were like."

The American Mountain Men

Two Bears and others like him who are totally mesmerized by those early mountaineers are drawn to The American Mountain Men. Whether you consider them the elite, hard-core, or lunatic fringe, the fellows of the AMM are definitely maximum 'skinners. Just look down the list of requirements for the third, or *Hiverano*, degree of membership:

1. Must have at least three full years of membership in AMM.

Maximum 'skinner Michael "Two Bears" Hughes: all the trappings of a free trapper, including an unquenchable thirst for adventure.

1. Must have at least three full years of membership in AMM.

2. Must have a full set of hand-cut and -sewn clothing and handmade accoutrements. These must be researched for authenticity of the 1800–1840 period.

3. Must spend at least three days and two nights totally alone under primitive conditions and *aux aliments du pays* ["off the nourishment of the land"].

4. Must have spent an accumulative time of two or more weeks in the wilderness under primitive conditions in the company of no more than one other member. Each stay must be at least three full days and two full nights.

5. Must have spent at least one full week in a primitive encampment in the company of other members.

6. Must be able to demonstrate the skills needed for primitive survival in the wilderness of his area and must be willing to teach said skills to other members.

7. Must be able to demonstrate trapping ability using steel traps, snares and traps made from natural materials found in his area.

8. Must be able to show ability to tan or Indian-dress hides.

9. Must be able to demonstrate ability to track man or animal under wilderness conditions.

10. Must be able to converse using Plains Indian hand talk.

11. Must have served as a booshway for at least two activities of the AMM.

12. Must have spent at least two days and one night in a primitive camp during each season of the year.

13. Must have made a study of the life style of the mountain men (or frontiersmen or American Indian) before 1840 and must submit a report of this study to the association *Capitaine*.

14. Must have hunted for and killed at least one game or fur animal with a muzzleloading firearm or primitive bow and must have used the skin and/or meat for food, clothing and/or accoutrements. The hunt must be from a strictly primitive camp, accomplished under primitive conditions and within the limits of local game laws.

15. Must have spent at least five days traveling on foot, snowshoe, canoe and/or horseback.

Maximum 'skinner Dan "Buffler" Brewer and Star. Trail riding with primitive tack (note Santa Fe saddle) is becoming a popular part of the rendezvous scene. On the trail, Buffler packs lightweight foods like jerky and hardtack. Water is where he finds it.

a) One method or a combination may be used.

b) Bullboat may be used in place of canoe.

c) You are expected to gain as much distance as possible.

d) This trip must be under primitive conditions, taking nothing that would not have been available to the mountain man between 1820–1840. Rifle, hunting bag, powder horn and knife must be along.

16. Must be able to demonstrate the ability to properly pack a horse, or a canoe, or a man for distance travel under possible adverse conditions.

17. Must be able to properly skin an animal and prepare the skin for market.

18. Must be able to properly field dress a game animal under primitive conditions.

19. Must be able to cook a meal of meat using only the meat, fire, a knife, and materials found in nature.

20. Must be able to start a fire in wet as well as dry weather using flint and steel or fire drill using tinder and wood found under natural conditions.

Other Historical "Activists"

Some 'skinners dabble in several historical periods. They may be mountain men on the weekend of a big rendezvous or primitive shoot, and Civil War soldiers or 1880s gunslingers the following weekend. As *Muzzleloader* publisher Oran Scurlock said, there's something for everyone—and there's no reason (save the very good ones of time and money) why a body can't sample a little of any or all of it.

A good many of my mountain man friends, Col. Two Bears among them, are also commissioned officers in the Texas Army. The Army has nothing *but* officers—all colonels except for commanding Gen. Carroll "Curly" Lewis. Governor Preston Smith reactivated the state's military forces in 1969, calling upon muzzleloading enthusiasts to dress in circa-1836 clothing and fire blank salutes and historical celebrations. The Army even has a pair of working cannon which stand in for the Twin Sisters, the field pieces used at the Battle of San Jacinto where ragtag Texian forces routed Santa Anna's veteran troops and won independence for the Republic of Texas. That army was hastily formed of farmers and hunters and townsmen, so at today's recreations you might see any manner of dress from a full suit of skins to frock coat and top hat. It's great fun with the serious purpose of reminding Texans—of which so many are transplants these days—that the ground we live on was earned with blood.

There are similar reenactment groups all over the nation, each drawing

The Texas Army recreates the defeat of Santa Anna at the foot of the San Jacinto Monument near Houston, site of the original battle.

their spark from local or regional history. The North-South Skirmish Association and the Brigade of the American Revolution organized large-scale reenactments in the East. Westerners have outfits like the National Outlaw and Lawman Association to help them recreate the days of the shootists.

The Indian Wars period of the 1870s has its aficionados, who dress and arm themselves as cavalry troopers. And the other side gets its due in the many groups of Indian hobbyists, including many non-Indians, who are typically more interested in preserving native culture in the form of dances and ceremonies than in smoking up the landscape with black powder.

Hunting and Trapping

Virtually all buckskinners shoot muzzleloaders. And we know by the popularity of guns like the Thompson/Center Hawken that the majority of muzzleloading enthusiasts are hunters. Ergo, it stands to reason that the average 'skinner is also a black-powder hunter.

But the two pursuits don't automatically mix. The question arises: Should you take advantage of modern innovations like the new, more efficient conical bullets, Pyrodex, plastic quick-loading devices for carrying premeasured charges, and improved sighting equipment? Or should you strive for authenticity in your hunting, too?

John Wootters, a nationally known gun writer who enjoys muzzleloading, answers this way: "I think this strict adherence to authenticity is fine fun at a rendezvous, where you can't hurt anything. But when you're hunting, you're going to be shooting at something that bleeds and feels pain, and you have the responsibility to do that as efficiently as possible, within the self-imposed limitation of hunting with a muzzleloader. It's not like shooting at frying pans and ax heads.

"Besides," Wootters adds with a wry smile, "peel a buckskinner and you'll usually find Fruit of the Loom."

Wootters, who owns a ranch in the magical brush country of southern Texas, frequently hunts in a controlled situation where each hunter knows where all the other hunters are. So while he doesn't feel the need to go strictly primitive, he does like to wear a buckskin hunting shirt for its comfort and quietness—and, I suspect, for its romantic link with the past.

Writer John Wootters, author of the classic *Hunting Trophy Deer*, likes to do his blackpowder hunting in a combination of buckskins and jeans. Many 'skinners, too, opt for hunting togs that are a blend of the primitive and modern.

John Baird, founder of the National Association of Primitive Riflemen and as 'skinner as they come, cautions against wearing primitive garb in less-controlled situations.

"It's not so bad in primitive-only seasons where everybody knows everybody else is hunting with a muzzleloader and may be in skins—that's great," Baird said. "But many states have mixed seasons where you have modern hunters out there with scope-sighted rifles and everything. The first year I hunted in Montana, I hunted in buckskins, gray blanket coat with a couple of feathers in my hat, and the deer thought I was another deer—which is an indication the *hunters* would probably have thought I was a deer. Since then I have followed the flame-orange thing. It doesn't lend much to the romance, but it's safer."

A couple of fellows I know thought enough of the romance of buckskins to wear them deer hunting in one of the national forests of eastern Texas. They came across another pair in blaze orange toting scoped bolt-actions and were lucky enough to spot them first. The 'skinners stepped out into a clearing and hailed the startled deer hunters.

"Ye pilgrims be knowin' how to find Houston?" one mountain man asked.

The reply was a while in coming since the hunters in orange apparently

Maximum 'skinners spend a lot of time at the range, brushing up their skills for primitive shoots and hunting season.

knew nothing of buckskinning and therefore had no idea anybody still stalked the woods dressed like that. Finally, one of them said, "Take that road back yonder over to the west until you hit Interstate 45, then straight south. It's a big place, you can't miss it."

"*Place?*" the 'skinner said. "We be lookin' fer Houston th' *man!* Heered tell he's gatherin' up a volunteer army."

The story is that one of the hunters looked at his watch. Watches nowadays have so many gizmos on them that maybe he was assuring himself it was the year he thought it was. More likely he was simply confused and it was an automatic reaction. Neither of them recovered quickly enough to say another word before the 'skinners melted back into the forest.

I realize I'm not helping you decide your path between primitive and modern by bouncing back and forth between the danger and fun of going primitive. The truth is my own allegiance to primitive gear bounces around to suit my mood. And that, I believe, is how it should be. I've enjoyed slipping quietly beneath a leafy canopy in moccasins with a full horn and a pouch at my side. If the hunting is going to be an extension of a primitive outing—and on what I deem to be safe ground—I'll jump at the chance to go in skins. But if we're going to have to drive around a lot, or if I'm in a group that insists on having the amenities of the twentieth century, then I'm going to wear my Fred Bear hat, L.L. Bean boots, and stuff my pockets with premeasured charges.

You must find your own path.

Since the original mountain men were trappers by occupation, some 'skinners take up the pursuit of furbearers as an extension of their hobby. It can be a profitable one, too.

Every Saturday morning during the trapping season, at an abandoned gas station in a small town near my home, there is a replay of those original rendezvous, with a buyer for a fur company meeting trappers. Elsewhere in the state, an organization of trappers holds a big fur auction several times during the season. Prices vary from year to year, but a good trapper who works at it can certainly count on earning enough in a season to buy a fine rifle or maybe a Santa Fe saddle, besides experiencing, as Col. Two Bears says, the other eleven months of the mountain man's life.

You can still find the old-style long-spring traps the mountaineers used, but the modern coil-spring traps are favored, even by 'skinners, because they're more compact and fit better into the hollows of logs and trees and such.

Fur Trapping in North America by Steven M. Geary is a good primer, and *Trapper* magazine (Box 550, Sutton, Nebraska 68979) will put you in touch with trappers' organizations such as Fur Takers of America or the National Trappers Association, Inc.

Hoping for a raccoon, Michael "Two Bears" Hughes uses leaves to mask a spring set. Most mountain men were trappers, so some 'skinners take up trapping to recapture the spirit of their lonely existence when they weren't at rendezvous.

Traveling Primitive

I get tremendous satisfaction out of packing into a primitive outing by primitive means. It's as though the distance you travel creates a real barrier against the realities of the twentieth century. Gone is the temptation to carry an ice chest, or to stroll over to the car for more water. It really generates a sense of going back in time.

The simplest way is to get yourself a pack basket and hoof it. The water problem becomes critical here, and you just about have to select a campsite where some is available, or cache it there in advance.

For those who have the necessary waterways, a canoe is a wonderful machine. A genuine birchbark would be the first choice, of course, but the next best thing authenticity-wise is a wood frame covered in canvas and lacquered. *Mechanix Illustrated* used to have plans for such boats back in the 1950s, but I undertand they're all gone now. A trip to a big library might prove fruitful, though. To appease their sense of the aesthetic without going quite that far, some 'skinners paint their aluminum or fiberglass canoes in a birchbark pattern.

Personally, I don't find any of that necessary. Function is more important than looks to me. My Topsiders boat shoes would never pass muster at a rendezvous, but there's not much difference between them and a pair of hard-soled Assiniboine moccasins in function. There is, on the other foot, a rather substantial difference in function between a canoe paddle and an Evinrude, between flint and steel and a Cricket lighter, between a candle lantern and a Coleman lantern. I say leave that stuff behind, but feel free to wear your plastic ball cap and paddle your plastic boat.

We know the mountain men did some traveling in the upper Missouri system by boat, and there were times when they had to travel afoot. But given a choice, the true mountain man would never walk *or* paddle when he could ride.

"The western mountain man was a horse-mounted man," said Walter J. McCurdy, former editor of the AMM's *Tomahawk and Long Rifle*, "so a lot more people are beginning to incorporate that into the rendezvous. I see a lot more guys either riding in or bringing their horses in by trailer."

"When the first trapper and trader came west overland on horses, they were probably using the civilian saddles of this period which were not too unlike some European saddles," says Bob Schmidt, a student and maker of old-time saddles. "As these saddles were lost, stolen or wore out, they were replaced with the Indian-style saddles which were called squaw, Crow or prairie chicken snare saddles. The Indian pad saddle was also used.

"When the trapper worked his way southwest, he probably would have come in contact with the Mexican or Santa Fe saddle. Most people today

A canoe is wonderful for getting into areas unspoiled by motorized outdoorsmen. This "wilderness" setting is only thirty miles from downtown Houston.

consider the so-called Santa Fe type as a kind of stereotype with the large platter-like horn and hand-holds in the cantle. The large, flat horn is actually from the decade following the last rendezvous. Paintings of the early era, such as those by Alfred Jacob Miller and other artists, show relatively small horns on saddles."

Schmidt builds saddles, both Indian and Spanish styles, to order. You can contact him by writing White Buffalo Leather Shop, 1224 N.E. Hamilton Heights Road, Corvallis, Montana 59828.

The near-100-year-old firm of El Paso Saddlery Co. will whomp you up a southwestern-style saddle to order. Their saddle, available with the big square *mochilla*, or covering, popular during the era, comes with a flat horn, high cantle, and wooden "bell" stirrups. Send $2 to Box 27194, El Paso, Texas 79926 for a catalogue.

Three good sources of information about the saddles of the Western Fur Trade Era are *The Horse in Blackfoot Indian Culture*, by John C. Ewers; *The Mystic Warriors of the Plains*, by Thomas E. Mails; and *Man Made Mobile: Early Saddles of Western North America*, Richard E. Ahlborn, editor.

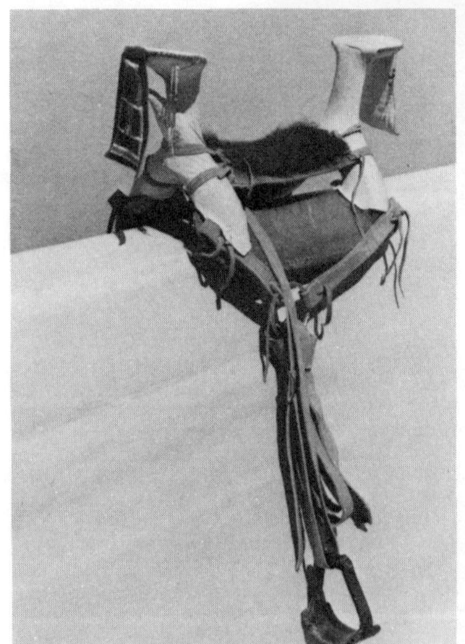

Indian-style saddles made by Bob Schmidt: *top*, Crow or squaw saddle; *bottom*, two styles of prairie chicken snare saddle. (Photos by Bob Schmidt)

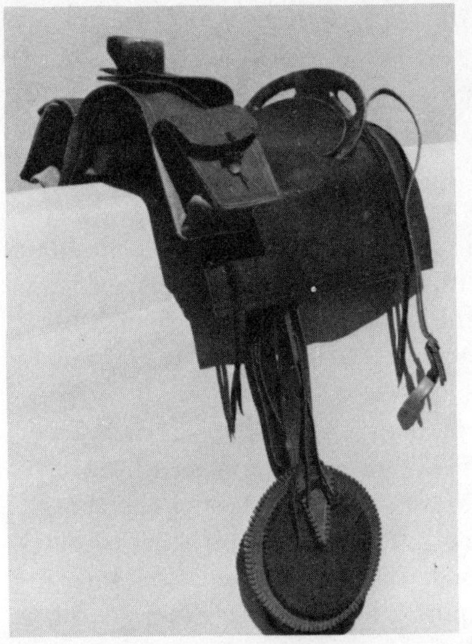

Left, early Santa Fe saddle; *right*, post-1840 Santa Fe saddle with buffalo-hide *mochila*. (Photos by Bob Schmidt)

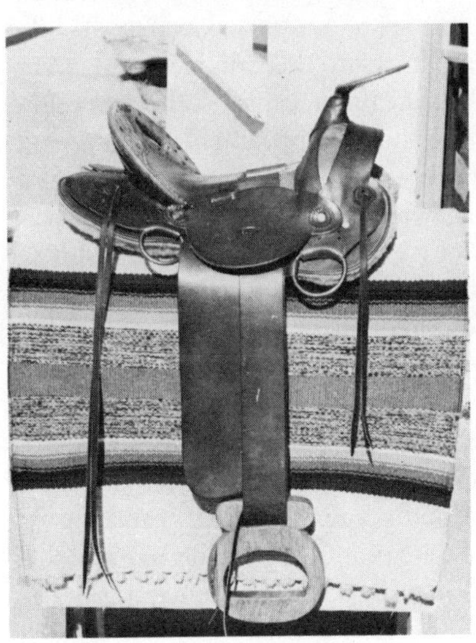

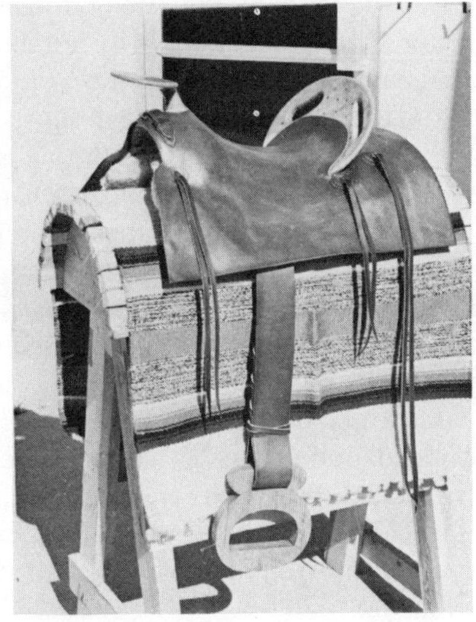

Two saddles made by El Paso Saddlery Co.: *left*, early southwestern saddle; *right*, "Mountain Man" saddle. (Courtesy of The El Paso Saddlery Co.)

Reincarnation and Medicine

I don't know whether buckskinning attracts people who believe in reincarnation or buckskinning causes people to believe in reincarnation, but it seems to me an inordinately high number do honestly harbor suspicions that they have seen all this before.

Although I have no personal feelings one way or the other about reincarnation, I certainly have no intention of making light of it. Let him who is without weird thoughts cast the first stone. In the minds of our thoroughly modern friends, neighbors, and relatives, all us buckskinners are weird.

The most prevalent symptom (and perhaps least "weird" in the eyes of mainstream America these days) is the adoption of a nineteenth-century philosophy. 'Skinners are generally conservative, the last of the rugged individualists. How could you expect otherwise in a hobby that eschews modern conveniences and places a high value on self-reliance and improvisation? Again, it's hard to determine whether buckskinning attracts self-reliant people or causes them to become that way. A combination of the two is my guess.

But there is also a certain religiosity some 'skinners develop that can be traced directly to the strong Indian influence in buckskinning. While many 'skinners undoubtedly establish altars in their lodges and wear medicine bags around their necks for the sake of pageantry, others develop a true feeling for the spiritual values these things represent. It is not—and I can only speak for myself in this regard—a denial of Christianity, but a supplement to it. The Indian "charms," or medicine, aren't themselves objects of worship, but rather symbols of a greater power. It's the result of simultaneously immersing yourself in nature and making yourself aware of how the Indians viewed the phenomena of nature. You might come to appreciate the Indian's nature-based religion without coming into conflict with your own.

Let's take the matter of medicine, or "charms." Say for example you're camped out during a severe thunderstorm. You're awed, maybe even frightened, by the power displayed. Suddenly your skin tingles and the air is crackly. Then the whole world seems to explode. Lightning has struck a tree nearby. You're unharmed, but it was a singular experience to say the least.

A charred fragment of bark from that tree would make an interesting keepsake, and anyone would be tempted to save it. But while the average Joe would treat it as a conversation piece, the 'skinner, with his knowledge of Indian religion, might tuck it away and keep it, well, sort of *sacred*—a reminder of a moving, and highly personal, experience. That piece of bark would be his medicine.

I think we non-Indians are too quick to explain away things like

Old-time Indian religion lives in the heart of many a 'skinner. In the broad Indian pantheon, the owl was especially respected and thought by some cultures to have the power to cure ailments.

lightning bolts in terms of physics and chemistry. It depersonalizes the experience. I was in a marathon canoe race once where we paddled around the clock, snatching a thirty-minute nap here and there. As night fell on the third day, I started hallucinating. The willows on the banks turned vividly into pre-Columbian statues and great, gray bas-relief walls. The most persistent vision was of a huge, round head I later matched with an example of ancient Olmec art. I knew while it was happening that I was hallucinating and that fatigue was causing it, but I couldn't blink it away. Nor did I really want to. It was fun.

I realize those images were planted in my head, probably while I once idly thumbed through a *National Geographic*. But the hallucination still created a powerful, and pleasant, memory. And I can understand why the Indians would undertake the rigors of a vision quest and how, without the benefit of physics or chemistry or psychology to ruin it for them, they could attach such significance to their visions.

I'm not suggesting you must believe in reincarnation or seek visions to be a maximum 'skinner. You only have to feel a need for more contact with nature and the primitive life than you experience at regular rendezvous.

You'll find your own way to satisfy that need.

Bibliography

Abel, Annie Heloise, ed. *Journal at Fort Clark, 1834–39*. Pierre, S.D.: Department of History, State of South Dakota, 1932. (Journal of Francis Chardon.)

Ahlborn, Richard E., ed. *Man Made Mobile: Early Saddles of Western North America*. Washington, D.C.: Smithsonian Institution Press, 1980.

Bronson, L.D. *Early American Specs*. Glendale, Calif.: The Occidental Publishing Company, 1974.

Camp, Charles L. *George Yount and His Chronicles of the West*. Denver: The Old West Publishing Company, 1966.

————— *James Clyman, 1792–1881*. Portland: Champoeg Press, 1960.

Campbell, Robert. *The Rocky Mountain Letters of Robert Campbell*. New York: Frederick W. Beinecke, 1955.

Carter, H.L. *"Dear Old Kit": The Historical Christopher Carson*. Norman: University of Oklahoma Press, 1968.

Chittenden, H.M. *The American Fur Trade of The Far West*, 2 vols. New York: Barnes & Noble, n.d.

Cleland, R.G. *This Reckless Breed of Men*. Albuquerque: University of New Mexico Press, 1976. (The southwestern fur trade.)

Coues, Elliot, ed. *Forty Years a Fur Trader on the Upper Missouri: The Personal Narrative of Charles Larpenteur, 1833–1872*, 2 vols. New York: F.P. Harper, 1898.

DeVoto, Bernard. *Across the Wide Missouri*. Boston: Houghton Mifflin Co., 1947. (Includes paintings and sketches by Alfred Jacob Miller.)

Ellison, William H., ed. *The Life and Adventures of George Nidever (1809–1883)*. Berkeley: University of California Press, 1937.

Ewers, John C. *The Horse in Blackfoot Indian Culture*. Washington, D.C.: Smithsonian Institution Press, 1969.

Fadala, Sam. *Black Powder Hunting*. Harrisburg, Pa.: Stackpole Books, 1978.

Fecteau, Susan. *Primitive Indian Dresses*. Edited by Vickie Zimmer. Distributed by Lance Grabowski, RD. 2, Hudson, N.Y. 12534.

Flayderman, Norm. *Flayderman's Guide to Antique American Firearms and Their Values*, 2nd ed. Northfield, Ill.: DBI Books, n.d.

Geary, Steven M. *Fur Trapping in North America.* San Diego: A.S. Barnes & Company, Inc., 1981.

Gowans, Fred R. *Rocky Mountain Rendezvous: A History of the Fur Trade Rendezvous 1825–1840.* Provo, Utah: Brigham Young University Press, 1976.

Grant, Madison. *The Kentucky Rifle Hunting Pouch.* n.p.: Madison Grant, 1977. Available from Track of the Wolf, Box Y, Osseo, Minnesota 55369.

Gray, William H. *A History of Oregon, 1792–1849.* Portland: Harris & Holman, 1870.

Hacker, Rick. *The Muzzleloading Hunter.* Tulsa: Winchester Press, 1981.

Haines, Aubrey L., ed. *Journal of a Trapper.* Portland: Oregon Historical Society, 1955. (Journal of Russell Osborne.)

Hanson, Charles E., Jr. *The Northwest Gun.* Nebraska State Historical Society Publications in Anthropology, vol. 2. Lincoln: Nebraska State Historical Society, 1955.

Hanson, James Austin, and Wilson, Kathryn J. *The Mountain Man's Sketch Book*, vol. 1. Chadron, Neb.: The Fur Press, 1979.

———— *The Mountain Man's Sketch Book*, vol. 2 Chadron, Neb.: The Fur Press, 1978.

Josephy, Alvin M., Jr. *The Indian Heritage of America.* New York: Alfred A. Knopf, 1968.

Laubin, Reginald and Gladys. *The Indian Tipi: It's History, Construction, and Use.* New York: Ballantine Books, 1977.

Mails, Thomas E. *Dog Soldiers, Bear Men and Buffalo Women.* Englewood Cliffs, N.J.: Prentice-Hall, 1973.

———— *The Mystic Warriors of the Plains.* Garden City, N.Y.: Doubleday, 1972.

McKay, Douglas. *The Honourable Company.* Freeport, N.Y.: ARNO, 1970. (The Hudson's Bay Company.)

Morgan, Dale. *Jedediah Smith and the Opening of the West.* Lincoln: University of Nebraska Press, 1969.

Murdock, George P., and O'Leary, Timothy J. *Ethnographic Bibliography of North America*, 4th ed., 5 vols. New Haven: Human Relations Area Files Press, n.d.

Nonte, George C., Jr. *Black Powder Guide*, 2nd ed. South Hackensack, N.J.: Stoeger Publishing Company, 1980.

Ogden, Peter Skene. *Snake Country Journals*, 3 vols. London: The Hudson's Bay Record Society, 1950–1971.

Oglesby, R.E. *Manuel Lisa and the Opening of the Missouri Fur Trade.* Norman: University of Oklahoma Press, 1963.

Orchard, William C. *The Technique of Porcupine Quill Decoration Among The Indians of North America.* New York: Museum of the American Indian, Heye Foundation, 1971.

Oswald, Delmont, ed. *The Life and Adventures of James P. Beckworth as Told to Thomas D. Bonner.* Lincoln: University of Nebraska Press, 1972.

Phillips, Paul C. *The Fur Trade.* Norman: University of Oklahoma Press, 1961.

———— *Life in the Rocky Mountains: A Diary of Wanderings on the Sources of the Rivers Missouri, Columbia and Colorado from February, 1830, to November, 1835.* Denver: The Old West Publishing Company, 1940. (Diary of W.F. Ferris.)

Quaife, Milton, ed. *Kit Carson's Autobiography.* Lincoln: University of Nebraska Press, 1935.

Rawling, Gerald. *The Pathfinders*. New York: The Macmillan Co., 1964.

Ross, Marvin C., ed. *The West of Alfred Jacob Miller: 1837*. Norman: University of Oklahoma Press, 1951.

Rounds, Glen, ed. *Mountain Men: George Frederick Ruxton's First Hand Accounts of Fur Trappers and Indians in the Rockies*. New York: Holiday House, 1966.

Russell, Carl P. *Firearms, Traps, & Tools of the Mountain Men*. Albuquerque: University of New Mexico Press, 1979.

Ruxton, George Frederick. *Life in the Far West*. Norman: University of Oklahoma Press, 1964.

Scurlock, William H., ed. *The Book of Buckskinning*. Texarkana, Tex.: Rebel Publishing Company, n.d.

Steiger, Brad. *Medicine Power: The American Indian's Revival of His Spiritual Heritage and Its Revelance for Modern Man*. Garden City, N.Y.: Doubleday, 1974.

Storm, Hyemeyohsts. *Seven Arrows*. New York: Ballantine Books, 1977.

Sunder, J.E. *Bill Sublette, Mountain Man*. Norman: University of Oklahoma Press, 1959.

Thorp, Raymond W., and Bunker, Robert. *Crow Killer: The Saga of Liver-Eating Johnson*, 2nd ed., rev. Bloomington and London: Indiana University Press, 1969.

Victor, Frances Fuller. *The River of the West*. Hartford: Columbian Book Company, 1870. (Joe Meek's story.)

Wagner, W.F., ed. *Adventures of Zenas Leonard, Fur Trader and Trapper 1831–36*. Cleveland: The Burrows Brothers Company, 1904.

Weber, David J. *The Taos Trapper*. Norman: University of Oklahoma Press, 1971.

White, George M. *Craft Manual of North American Indian Footwear*. Ronan, Mont.: George M. White, 1969. Available through Tandy Leathercraft stores or from George M. White, Box 365, Ronan, Montana 59864.

Wigginton, Eliot, ed. *Foxfire 3*. Garden City, N.Y.: Anchor Press/Doubleday, 1975. (Includes folk methods of tanning hides.)

——— *Foxfire 5*. Garden City, N.Y.: Anchor Press/Doubleday, 1979. (Contains a section on muzzleloading.)

Wildschut, William, and Ewers, John C. *Crow Indian Beadwork: A Description and Historical Study*. New York: Museum of the American Indian, 1973.

Wilson, Kathryn J., and Hanson, James A. *Feminine Fur Trade Fashions*. Chadron, Neb.: The Fur Press, 1976.

Woodward, Arthur, ed. *The Autobiography of a Mountain Man, 1805–1889*. Pasadena: G. Dawson, 1948. (Autobiography of Stephen Hall Meek.)

Young, F.G., ed. *A Record of Two Expeditions for the Occupation of the Oregon Country, with Maps, Introduction and Index*. Sources of the History of Oregon, Vol. 1. Eugene: University Press, 1899.

Index